Pedro Bay, Alaska – Past, Present, and Distant Memories

WALTER'S STORY

BARBARA JACKO ATWATER

PO Box 221974 Anchorage, Alaska 99522-1974
books@publicationconsultants.com—www.publicationconsultants.com

ISBN 978-1-59433-308-8
eBook ISBN 978-1-59433-309-5

Library of Congress Catalog Card Number: 2012941976

Manufactured in the United States of America.

Dedication

I dedicate this to my mother,
Dolly Foss Jacko.

Contents

Acknowledgements

This project would not have been possible without Walter's complete cooperation, wonderful memory and sheer joy in storytelling. His daughter Ruth Andree's enthusiasm, encouragement and full support also helped me tremendously. She was always so helpful with the coordination of our visits. Thanks to my mother, Dolly Foss Jacko and Mary Jensen for their willingness to answer my questions and share photos with me.

Thanks to Jeanne Schaaf and the staff at Lake Clark National Park Service in Anchorage for helping me with photos and background information. My thanks go to all those who donated their photos to the park service. It is quite a wonderful repository of old photos. Thanks also to Clarence Baak, Violet Wilson and Marjorie Jensen for photos.

Thanks to Debbie Sonberg for her help with my photoshop issues. I thank Hazel Schofield for reading my document for meaning and giving me instructive feedback.

Many thanks go to Katherine Arndt. Her research provided much background history for Walter's Story.

Thanks to my son Ethan for his patience with me and accompanying me on our many visits to Walter in Homer.

Finally, I thank my husband, Steve for his help with the editing, with help when I got stuck on phrasing and his encouragement by telling me that this was a good story – a story worth telling.

Barbara Jacko Atwater

Introduction

In 1986 while taking a class I started a family tree of the original families of Pedro Bay. Since then I have wanted to do something about the history of the northeast area of Iliamna Lake, where my home, Pedro Bay, is located. Hearing stories of the various characters that had lived in the area was always intriguing to me. Over the years I made notes, recorded interviews, and collected historical material having to do with the area. It wasn't long before I had a briefcase and head full of notes that desperately needed organizing and telling.

I am not sure when I decided that accomplishing this telling would be best done through the story of one person. I think it came about gradually as I started to spend more and more time listening to Walter and Annie Johnson. Choosing Walter as that one person was, I think, natural since he is such a great storyteller and also because of his unique childhood. Of his siblings, even though he was the youngest Walter was the only one fluent in the Dena'ina language and knowledgeable of so many of the old Dena'ina stories. This came from growing up alone with his mother, who spoke only Dena'ina in the home and spent a lot of time passing on Dena'ina lore to Walter.

When I first approached Walter about this project he told me I was too late. He was referring to his other book *Sukdu Nel Nuhtghelnek I'll Tell You A Story*, done by James Kari of the University of Alaska Fairbanks published in 2004. I was unaware of this book and felt discouraged. It is quite wonderful, by the way, if you have not read it. In her forward to the book *Ruthie Andree*, Walter's daughter, actually gave me an opening with her statement. "Another book in itself could be made from Dad's stories just about checking the trap line during the winters." So I persisted and with some encouragement from Ruthie, Walter decided perhaps there was more to tell.

Once that decision was made, we started the interviews. While interviewing, transcribing the interviews and organizing the information chronologically, I found I had another decision to make. At first, I thought I would interview others, Walter's family and friends, to add to the story. However, it soon became clear to me that this was Walter's story.

Walter lived his life in such an engaging way. Lacking any formal education, he navigated through the intricacies of modern life with a wonderful patience and persistence. He never shied away from attempting things that he didn't know about; he built cabins, installed engines in boats, relocated his family to California, and visited Hawaii for several months with his wife Annie. He accomplished all these things and more on his own.

Gathering the information for this book has spanned several years. Walter would often revisit a subject and of course he would tell the stories as he remembered them not as they happened. As a result I had to reorder, reorganize and often reword a lot of what he said, trying to maintain his voice throughout. I hope I have been successful in this.

The "Distant Memories" are what I believe to be some of the oral history of the Dena'ina people of this particular area. These are all Walter's memories, passed on to him from his mother and other elders.

I do not know the Dena'ina language and there were times when it was hard to find the correct English for a Dena'ina word Walter used. In these cases I thought it is best to use the Dena'ina word, however, sometimes I could not even find the Dena'ina word. One of these was the word Walter used for the invisible people. Kari has several terms for this in his *Dena'ina Topical Dictionary* but none of them seemed to fit what Walter was using so I decided a blank was the best way to deal with this word.

I should also mention the fireball or ball lightening stories. Walter did talk of these often but I chose not to include them here since they are covered in some detail in the Kari book. There is even an illustration of Walter's description on the cover of that book.

In the endnotes and appendices I included further information on topics and individuals that Walter either did not mention or could not recall. It is here the notes and information I had been gathering and felt needed sharing can be found. Here also is the additional information I gathered through research and from conversations with others of the area. Because I tried to keep in mind that the reader would most likely be connected in some way to Walter's story, I also included several genealogies. Hopefully, these will help some of you clarify your connections to the area.

Any errors found in this book are mine. I have tried to be as diligent as possible to be accurate in this telling but the possibility of error is always there. So I do apologize if something seems glaringly wrong. Please feel free to contact me if you have a correction or clarification.

While at a gathering, my brother once looked directly at me and stated, "Someone needs to write a history of this area." Well, Norman, here is one version of that history.

Barbara Jacko Atwater
December 2011

Timeline

1750-2009

1750s	Pedro Bay area occupied by the Dena'ina.[1]
1778	Stepan Alekseev Rykhterov is born in Russia. He is Walter's Great Great Grandfather. Died August 3, 1847. Marina Mikhailovna, Aleut, is born in Unalaska. She is Walter's Great Great Grandmother and Stepan's wife. Died January 3, 1856.
1797	The Russian explorer, Filipp Kashevenov traveled over the Iliamna Bay Portage. He described it as being well traveled. He also noted that there was a small fortification of the Lebedov Fur Company.[2]
1799	Alexander Baranov (1746-1819), the first Russian governor of Alaska, received news that a Russian establishment at Iliamna had been destroyed and the Russians massacred.[3]
1813	Savva #1 (Savelii) Stepan Rykhterov is born in Kodiak to Stepan Rykhterov and his wife Marina Mikhailovna, of Unalaska. Savva is Walter's Great Grandfather. He died November 24, 1884 at age 87.
1818	The Russian Explorer Petr Korsakovskiy traveled up Iliamna Lake. He stopped at a village in the area of Pedro Bay. He hired a local to take him to the settlement on Iliamna River to meet a Russian trader there by the name of Rodionov.[4]

1840s	Rikterovs were living in the Old Iliamna Village.[5]
August 23 1842	Savva Rykhterov (age 29) marries Glikeriia Mylykhchtaitna (born 1813), a Kenaika of Kultuk settlement. These were Walter's great grandparents.
March 9 1851	Vasilii (William) Savvin Rykhterov is born to Savva Riktorov and his wife Glikeriia. William was Walter's grandfather. Savva is listed as the Iliamna Odinochka indicating he was a leader or manager of the village.[6]
1880	Anna born to Vasilii and Mariia Semenova in Old Iliamna Village. Anna is Walter's mother.[7]

1897-8	Lt. Hugh Rodman of the U.S. Navy and U.S. Coast and Geodesic Survey traveled into the Lake District via the Iliamna Trail. Some of his photos were printed in the Alaska Geographic Society's 1986 book called: *"Lake Clark, Lake Iliamna Country"*.
1906	Pedro Bay occupied by only one man – Old Man Pedro (Pedtrushko).
1909	First school opened in the Old Iliamna Village by H.O. Schaleben.
	Schaleben, a doctor, furnished medical services, while his wife Gertrude taught. Alex Flymn and some local men built the school building. The first year of attendance averaged 12 students with an enrollment of 27.[8]

1909-12 — Hannah Breece taught school in Old Iliamna Village.[9]

1916 — John Zug of the Board of Road Commissioners reconnoitered the trail between Iliamna Bay and the Old Iliamna Village and recommended that a 12-mile road be built.[10]

June 14 1922 — Walter Johnson was born at Kaskanak where his parents, Anna and Alf Johnson, were living at the time.[11]

1927 — Improvements made on the road between Iliamna Bay and Old Iliamna Village allowing the first horse drawn wagons to be used on the route. (Actually to Foss's Place which was across the river from the village.)

Foss's Landing on Iliamna River across from the Old Iliamna Village. Baard and Christina Foss with their sons, Sam and Hollie, raking hay. They owned horses so gathering hay was necessary for them.

(Courtesy of the NPS, Lake Clark National Park & Preserve. LACL 1300; H-703. Donated by Bert & Edna Foss, 1995.)

1927 — Walter's family moved to a house on Copper River, near Pope Vanoy, where they lived for about a year.

1928-9 — Walter's Dad Alf Johnson built the first house in Lonesome Bay.

1932 — School in Old Iliamna Village closed. The last teacher was Walter Johnston. He had a wife Nellie, son Frank, and daughter, Esther.

1936 — Walter's first year at Bristol Bay.

Holly Foss's home in 1952. Clarence Bakk said he arrived to find all the desks sitting on the porch. He also lived with Holly and Lagaria that year. Clarence said they always treated him with kindness.

(Photo courtesy of Clarence Bakk)

1937	The Iliamna Bay road was extended to Pile Bay, allowing direct access to Iliamna Lake.
Fall 1937	Walter's Mom died.
1937	The first house built in Pile Bay by Lyle Williams.[12]

Pile Bay in 1952 or 1953. Not sure who the person is.

(Courtesy of Clarence Bakk)

1940s	Foxy Kovoliak was the last person to move out of Old Iliamna Village.
Fall 1942	Walter made the trip to Anchorage via the Princess Pat with brother Nicolai Jensen and friend George Seversen.
May 16 1947	Walter married Annie (Mysee) Olsen and moved to Pedro Bay.
1949	Spent a winter in Loon Bay.
1951-2	Walter builds a house on the Kvichak River.
1951-52	First year of public school in Pedro Bay. Teacher John Coray.[13] Classes were held in the home of Sophie Foss.
1953	Walter sold house on Kvichak to Cecil of Naknek.

New classroom in new Pedro Bay School, 1953. Students: Bert Foss, Bertha Jacko, Victor Nicolai, Tom Foss, Freda Hedlund, Thelma Jacko, Sonny Hedlund, Pauline Kolyaha, Edna Foss, Irene Jensen, Johnny Foss.

(Courtesy of Clarence Bakk)

The new Pedro Bay school opened 1953 with Clarence Bakk as the teacher.

(Courtesy of Clarence Bakk)

1953-54	New school building opened up in Pedro Bay. Clarence Bakk was the first teacher. He taught the year before, in the home of Holly and Lagaria Foss.
1954	Moved to Homer, bought a piece of land, built a small house.
1954	Walter and family moved to Anchorage.
1958	Pile Bay abandoned as a community.
1962	Bought the *Hornet*, a commercial fishing boat. Moved to a suburb of Los Angeles, CA for 7 months.
1963	Moved back to Alaska for the fishing season and then to Pedro Bay. Bought brother Gus Jensen's house in Pedro Bay.

1967	Walter built a trapper's cabin on the Old Iliamna Village site.
1968	Moved to Tommy Pt.
1978	Moved back to Homer.
1995	Walter's 60th & final year of commercial fishing.[14]
2004	Walter's book came out. *Sukdu Nel Nuhtghelnek, I'll Tell You a Story,* Walter's recorded stories in Dena'ina with assistance of James Kari from University of Alaska, Fairbanks.
June 3 2008	Walter receives an award in Juneau at the 2007-2008 Awards Ceremony Honoring Alaska's Indigenous Literature (H.A.I.L).
January 8 2009	Annie Mycee Olsen Johnson, Walter's beloved wife, died.

The Russian Fort

"There was a Russian fort somewhere in Pedro Bay. A Russian boy was out on the lake ice-skating when this happened. The fort was attacked and destroyed, and all the Russians were killed. The boy was able to escape. He skated all the way up to the Old Iliamna Village. He was taken in there and hid by an Indian boy of the village. This Indian boy was his friend. The Russian boy then lived there and grew up.[1]

Origin of Old Iliamna Village

Due to the passage of time and lack of accurate record keeping the precise beginning of Old Iliamna Village is difficult to pinpoint. However, Russian Orthodox priests' journals and some Russian explorers' journals give some idea as to time, purpose, and individuals involved in the origin of the village.

One of the earliest mentions found is that of a Russian Explorer, Filipp Kashevenov. He traveled over the Iliamna Bay portage in 1797 and noted that, "it was well traveled, as there was on Iliamna a small fortification of the Lebedov Company."[2] It is not known if his referral to Iliamna is the Lake or the River. The Lebedov Company was a Russian Fur Trade Company in operation in the late 1700s, later joining with Lastochkin to become the Lebedev – Lastochkin Company, this eventually became the Russian Fur Company or Russian American Company (RAC).

The Russian Governor for Alaska, Baranof received news in the year 1799 that a Russian establishment at Iliamna had been destroyed and the Russians massacred. The reference to Iliamna would probably be Iliamna Lake. Oral history speaks of an event of this kind occurring in the area of present day Pedro Bay.

In the year 1818 a Russian explorer, Petr Korsakovskiiy traveled to Iliamna River to meet with a Russian Fur Trader by the name of Eremy Rodionov. In this journal it is stated that Rodionov was out of Tyonek. He had a summer camp on the Iliamna River and had his son with him. Korsakovskiiy had stopped at a settlement in the area of present day Pedro Bay and was "received ...well" by the Indians who lived there. They gave him the information on Rodionov. (*The Travel Journals of Petr Korsakovskiiy (1818)*)

Fr. Modestov states in a journal entry February 9, 1895 that, "This village had been founded by the Creole Savva Riktorov, who worked here as a trade agent for the

Winter scene of Old Iliamna Village.

(Alaska State Historical Library, The William Heald Collection, PCA 102-61.)

Russian company [RAC] and who was responsible for delivering supplies and goods from Kenai to Nushagak" (*Through Russian Orthodox Eyes*). Unfortunately, Modestov does not state the year that this occurred. Savva was born in Kodiak in 1813. He married a Glikeriia Mylykhchtaitna, an Indian of Kultuk settlement in 1842. Kultuk was a settlement in the Cook Inlet region. There are references to Savva as the "Iliamna odinochka Savva Riktorov" as early as 1847. In being referred to as the "baidarshchik of Iliamna odinochka" it is indicated that he is the leader of the community.

There are many other references to births and marriages occurring in and around the Iliamna odinochka by the person Savva #1 Stepan Rykterov, his brothers and children. This would indicate that the settlement there at Old Iliamna Village was well established by the late 1840s and early 1850s. There is also indication through the recordings of marriages and deaths that there was frequent

interaction between the Old Iliamna Village and communities along the Cook Inlet and the Kenai Peninsula.

From this information it would seem that the Old Iliamna Village was settled in the 1840s by Savva #1 Stepan Rykterov and his brothers, Savva #2 (1819 - 1882), and Ivan (1822 - 1888). The purpose of the settlement was for the Russian fur trade expansion into the Nushagak area. The Dena'ina who settled there were from the Pedro Bay area, Mulchatna area and the Cook Inlet Dena'ina villages.

However, there is indication that this area may have been settled even earlier or, there may have been settlements along the river by the local Dena'ina people at various times before the 1800s. See the Distant Memory "A Raid and a Rout". Also the report by the Russian Explorer Kashavenov indicated that the Iliamna Portage was well traveled in 1797. He stated that "the Kenaitsey (Dena'ina) use it ceaselessly going in both directions."

The War Party

A Distant Memory

"A large group of Dena'ina men prepared for a journey down the lake (Iliamna Lake). There were several large baidarka's (canoes) to be used. Each held six to eight men. The men had their weapons, bows and arrows, and spears. Their faces were painted. They took very little with them so as to be able to travel fast. This was to be a raid on a village down the lake."

Walter's Early Life

An Auspicious Beginning at Kaskanak

I was born at Kaskanak on June 14, 1922. This is a small river that enters the Kvichak about where the Kaskanak Flats are located. It is a couple miles below Igiugig. My parents were living in a cabin there at the time.

My Aunt Valun, Mom's youngest sister, was with Mom when I was born. My sister, Alma Jensen was there, too. I was the youngest of my mom's children.[1]

There were a bunch of loose dogs running around outside. They were the sled dogs, but they weren't tied up. Right after I was born, for some reason, Alma and Aunt Valun left Mom and ran out of the house. They left the door open and the dogs came into the house. They could have eaten me up. I guess Mom got them out somehow, but that was dangerous. I don't know what my sister and aunt were doing. Mom was not happy with them.

We lived there at Kaskanak for about five years. I don't remember too much of when we lived there in Kaskanak. The memories come and go.

This is one memory that I remember well because Hugh Millet would always tell me about it.[2]

One day he came down to visit us from his place up there at Millet's point, just west of Chekok. I was playing on the beach there on the riverbank. Well, he ran his boat up onto the beach and I was standing there looking up at his bow. Hugh walked up to the bow and yelled down at me. "Hello there, little Alf Johnson!" I said to him, "You go to hell!"

Hugh Millett in Naknek, AK in 1916.

(LACL 1300; H-564. NPS Lake Clark National Park and Preserve. Donated by Marie Millett in 1994.)

Walter's sister Alma with Mary Rickteroff behind her and Gladys Carlsen in her lap.

(Photo courtesy of Walter Johnson)

Boy, I don't know where I heard that word or why I said that, guess I didn't like being called little or Alf. But Hugh thought it was the funniest thing. He laughed and laughed. I was only four or five years old at the time. Yeah, he would always remind me of that.

Another memory I have was about the steam bath and the fire. You know how they used to build a big fire to heat the rocks for the steam. After the rocks are all hot and glowing, they would take two sticks and pile them inside the steam. Well, Mom and Dad did that. Then they went into the steam to take a bath. I was outside, playing. I was running around the fire and then I fell into it! It was full of red coals. I fell in with both my hands into the fire. Boy, I got out really quick but I yelled loud. I guess I ruined their steam. But, my hands were burned really badly. Dad put some kind of cream on them. I had to sleep in the windbreak for a long time because I needed to keep my hands cool. They healed. I don't even have any scars from that.

Our Winter Stay at Copper River

I can remember way back when I was five years old. We were now living at Copper River, over near Pope Vanoy - my mom and dad and myself. We lived in a house that belonged to a guy named Foster. I don't remember him, though. I think he was – outside, you know, out of state. We didn't stay there very long, just one winter.

I remember when the lake froze up. My mom used to like to fish, you know and there were a lot of trout and grayling at this place. Well, I went outdoors one day to find her. I liked to be by my mom, you know. That age I guess. She was out on the ice fishing. I went running out to her and I slipped down and hit my head on that ice. I didn't get knocked out or anything but I hit my head so hard I saw a flash of light.

I was wearing my cap and my hood, so I guess that saved my head from splitting. After I got up I went over to Mom and we went back to the house. That's all I remember of that.

Oh, there were a lot of echoes in that place, there in Copper River. The echoes were so clear. I knew where Buck and Frank and my brothers were living you know, up there at Old Iliamna Village. I knew where they were living and I thought they could hear me. So I would holler at them and tell them things. Then I would listen to the echo. I thought I was talking to them.

Lonesome Bay today. I tried to take this photo from the viewpoint Walter used in his illustration of Lonesome Bay as he remembered it when he lived there.

Yeah, I would sit outside and talk to my echo, thinking I was talking to them. That echo was really something, it was really clear.

This was in the fall time. The ice was just freezing over. These are some of my earliest memories.

Moving to Lonesome Bay

My dad named Lonesome Bay. I don't know why he picked a place that was so lonely. Well, there was a little game there, you know, like fox and stuff. He was the first one to build a house there. Mom had lived over in the Old Iliamna Village before she met my dad. They moved to Lonesome Bay after our winter at Copper River. It may be they moved there because it was closer to the Old Iliamna Village. I am not sure. Well, Dad built us a nice house there in Lonesome Bay.

A Woman Is Left Alone

A Distant Memory

"One time... a large group of Dena'ina from the ocean side (Tyonek) were traveling to Kijik; men, women, and children. They were traveling in the winter, early spring. These people were traveling from the ocean side. These Dena'ina people were on the lake — Lake Iliamna. Around midday they stopped on the ice to rest — it was early spring. A woman went up on the hillside to get new moss to change her baby. All the rest of the people were down on the ice.

While this woman was up on the hill a strange thing happened. All of a sudden there was an earthquake type explosion. All the people on the ice were like swallowed up. The ice seemed to just swallow them up. The lady that went up the hill for the moss was the only one that survived. She was left all alone.

People thought that maybe a big fish lived in the lake."

Left Alone

Dad Goes Away

Dad left in the spring of 1927. He left for Bristol Bay and never came back. I don't remember his leaving. I never saw him again until I was a teenager. He had built himself a place on Branch River, not far from Naknek. That was where he lived alone for the rest of his life. He died one winter when he fell through the ice.

Alf, my Dad had this little picture thing that you looked at pictures with. You held it up in front of your eyes to look at the pictures. He had all these pictures, boxes of them. My mom had this trunk full of his pictures. But it all got lost in that potlatch they had for her at Nondalton. People just took it all. I don't know why Alma didn't take that stuff and save it. My dad had all these pictures in there of his family in New York City. He was born in Estonia but grew up in New York City. It sure is too bad we lost all that.

I don't like to think of it.

Yeah, I don't have any memories of my dad in Lonesome Bay.

My brother Nicolai Jensen lived with us most of the time after Dad left. Nicolai was gone a lot though, you know, to go down to Bristol Bay to fish and to go trapping in the winter. My sisters, Alma and Virginia were with us some, too, but they were often over at the village to go to school. So we were alone a lot, Mom and I.

On Goose Bay

I think it was around 1925 when Charlie Roehl, Aunt Valun's husband decided to move from the Old Iliamna Village down the lake to Goose Bay.[1] Well, he actually built his first house closer to Chekok then moved it the next year to Goose Bay. He had my uncle William Mike[2] help him build a house down there. Then William Mike decided to build himself a house there, too. William Mike was married at that time to Annie John.[3]

After a while, Charlie's brothers, Henry and Fred, moved down to Goose Bay, too. Henry was married to Esther, the teacher Walter Johnston's daughter. Fred was married to Vera Rickteroff at that time. They were all sons of Fred Roehl, Sr.[4] He was the guy that owned the store there in the Old Iliamna Village. His kids all grew up there in the old village.

Billy Regan and his wife Dareya moved down there, too.[5]

Then Hugh Millet moved to Goose Bay. His Dad, Old Man Millet lived there above Millet's Point or Goose Bay. Hugh had operated the store in the Old Iliamna Village after Old Man Fred Roehl died. He, Hugh, had married Fred's daughter, Marie.

Billy Regan with Sam Foss, and unidentified boy at Foss's Landing. The horses belonged to the Fosses.

(Courtesy NPS. Lake Clark National Park & Preserve. LACL H-693. Donated by Bert and Edna Foss, 1995)

I guess he just got tired of living there in the Old Village and moved to be closer to his folks. Millet's Point is that point that juts out of Goose Bay.

Goose Bay was quite a little place for a while, but like Pile Bay it didn't last very long. It grew up fast and then it was gone. I think Charlie and Valun moved first. They moved down to Iliamna so their daughter Sophie could go to school there. Hugh lived there the longest, but then his wife, Marie decided the kids needed to go to school so she moved down to Dillingham. I guess Hugh went behind her. I don't know where he died.[6]

Grampa William Rickteroff Dies

One spring when Mom and I were visiting Goose Bay my grandpa, Old Man William died.[7] He was my mom's Dad. We were down there to visit and fish for trout. Mom liked to fish for trout and this was another good place for that. She would also visit Dareya, Billy Regan's wife. Dareya liked my mom and would always ask her to come and spend the night with her. She and her husband, Billy Regan had a house on Young's Creek. This was across the bay from Millet's Pt, there inside Goose Bay. Before that Billy Regan lived in the Old Iliamna Village. That was where he met and married Dareya. They lived in Goose Bay for a short while then moved down to Naknek.

Well, my grandpa was staying with my uncle William Mike. Grandpa was pretty sick and I guess we knew he was probably going to die. So we stayed with my aunt Valun there in Goose Bay until he died.

When Grandpa died they took him up to the Old Iliamna Village to bury him. I remember him just a little, because I was only six years old when he died.

William Rickteroff with his youngest daughter Valun.
(Courtesy of Walter Johnson)

Couldn't Keep My Mouth Shut!

I remember one winter we were sliding (sledding) in the Old Village. We would use cardboard paper. I must have been around seven or eight years old at this time. Anyway, we were sliding down this steep trail between the houses. Most of the homes at that time had these fences around their gardens by their houses. The gardens were fenced with posts and old gill net webbing, this was to keep the dogs out of the gardens.

Well, someone decided to put a piece of net across our sliding trail so we would have to duck under it. I was coming down that trail, laughing with my mouth wide open and I didn't duck under that net. Well, it caught my front tooth and ripped it right out of my head. Boy! That hurt! I was all bloody and crying. Annie Delkettie, Buck's sister, was playing with us then. She took me to her house and helped me get cleaned up. Boy, there was a lot of blood. After a while I felt better so I decided to slide some more. That net was still across the trail. Well, I got back on my cardboard and headed down the hill. I came sliding down real fast! I was laughing again, just couldn't stop because I was going so fast! Well, I didn't duck again or close my mouth and my other front tooth was ripped out! Boy, I just couldn't keep my mouth closed. Good thing they weren't my permanent teeth.

Yeah, we didn't have sleds back then, just cardboard. But I do remember Annie (Mysee) had a sled. Her Dad, Dick Mysee, made it for her. It was really nice. He put steel runners on it. Boy, that was a fast sled!

On *Ala*, Grasim Sours, my oldest brother

Grasim was born February 17, 1898. I don't know anything about his Dad, but I think he may have been from Nondalton. There was a Sours living down at Eagle Bay, but I don't know if he was related to Grasim, my brother.

Grasim went down to San Francisco to buy a boat. He used this boat to haul his own freight. He would buy a lot of stuff after fishing there in Bristol Bay for his little store. He didn't use the boat to commercial fish in. It was too long for that. So he would have to rent a company boat to use for commercial fishing. Grasim called his boat *The Advance*. Yeah, he used it to travel around on the Lake, haul his freight and travel down to Bristol Bay each fishing season.

Boy, that *Advance* was a nice boat. I used to like the bow of that boat. When you were in rough weather you could lie down on the bow and see those waves coming. You would go up and come down on those big waves and never get a drop of water on you. It really cut through the water nicely. It was a real sea boat.

One fall my brother, Grasim, moved from Lonesome Bay to Tommy Point. He built a house over there at Tommy Pt., so my mom and I lived with him there at

Tommy Pt. for a time. Grasim always had a little store, you know, wherever he lived he would have a store. He sold candies and things. People from around the Lake would come by to use his store. So when we were there at Tommy Pt. a lot of people came by to use his store.

We stayed there only for one winter, I think. Grasim liked to move around. He built himself a house at the Old Iliamna Village. In that picture of the old village with the airplane, the big house up in front is his. Then he had a house in Lonesome Bay. He was a pretty enterprising man. Yeah.

I think he was an alcoholic. He drank a lot. Grasim was married to Sophie Roehl. She was the daughter of Frederick and Mary Roehl. Grasim and Sophie never had any children. One fall Grasim got sick. He kind of got swollen in the abdomen, and he died shortly after. This was in Lonesome Bay. I think it was 1938. Grasim was only 40 years old then.

Sophie moved down to Goose Bay after Grasim died to stay with her sister, Marie Millet.

She then married Hans Seversen. After Seversen died she went on down to Dillingham and married Penman. She and Penman moved to live in Homer. They adopted her nephew Arthur Roehl because she had no children. Arthur was Fred and Vera Roehl's son.

Yeah, I don't even have a picture of Grasim. The only one I remember was lost at Mom's potlatch that they had up at Nondalton. We lost all of Mom's stuff at that potlatch.[8]

The Gravehouse

There is an old grave there, in Loon Bay just south of Tommy Pt. I don't know who died there but I used to be scared of that. We were living there for a while, you know with my brother Grasim. I was a little kid then. Mom would go fishing down the beach, you know. I used to go with her. We used a trail that went right by this grave. You know how a long time ago people built a little house on top of the grave? Well, that is how this one was. I never liked to go close to that grave. I was scared of it. I was afraid I might see that dead man in the cracks, you know. I thought the body was on top of the ground inside that little house.

Spring Trip to Iliamna Bay

One spring I remember going over to Iliamna Bay with my mom and I think it was Fedosia Carlson.[9] We walked over there to camp and get some clams in the early spring. When we got to Iliamna Bay we walked out around the point towards Cottonwood Bay and camped just around the point from Iliamna Bay. I remember it was good walking, when the tide was low, you know. This is where they camped a long time ago when the men hunted for fur otters. Well, we camped there for a few days. We didn't even have a tent. I guess we took a tarp or something like that to make a shelter. We walked so we couldn't pack much with us. When the weather got bad we walked back to Iliamna Bay.

Old Ed McKinnet was living there in Iliamna Bay then. He was doing the freight hauling over the road. He used a horse and wagon. Boy, that road was such a mess I sure don't know how he did it. You would get stuck often because it was just mud. Later he got an old truck that he used, but that got stuck, too.[10]

Well, there was a little cabin there in Iliamna Bay for people to use. It had a stove in it. So we stayed there until the weather got better. After the weather cleared we walked back over the road to the Old Iliamna Village. I must have been around 10 or 12 then, so this would have been in 1930 or 1932.

I remember being excited about going over to Iliamna Bay for the first time. People would tell me about how the water would go way out then come all the way back in. I really wanted to see that. Another thing was that the water was salty. That was the first thing I did when I got there the first time. I ran down to taste the water.

My Uncle Stephen and the Sledding Accident

I had an uncle named Stephen.[11] He broke his leg when he was a kid, maybe 6 or 7. My mom told me about that. There were a lot of kids in the Old Iliamna Village when this happened. My grandpa, Old William Rickteroff, had a sled with bone runners. I don't know what kind of a bone it was, might have been walrus. A bunch of the kids got together. They pulled William's sled up to just below the bridge, you know, that big sand bank? You know when you go up the river just past the Foss's there you come around a sharp bend, the oxbow bend. They hauled that sled all the way up that sand bank. It is a steep bank.

View of Old Iliamna Village
and the Oxbow
in the Iliamna River.
August 4-7, 1921.

Photo taken by Vreeland or MacNab.
(Courtesy NPS. Lake Clark National
Park & Preserve. LSCL H-841.)

Then they all got in that sled and went down that hill. Mom said they went so fast they could hardly breathe. They hit the ice and slid across the river so fast that they hit the bank on the other side very hard. That's where they piled up. The sled broke and there was no sliding after that. But that was where Stephen broke his leg. He was lame for the rest of his life and so he never married. I don't remember when he died.

On Joluk Zacarooski, Our Neighbor

There was a man named Joluk Zacarooski who lived in a little slough at the right side of the mouth of Pile River with his wife, son and daughter.[12] His house was a nice little place, had wallpaper on the inside walls. He even had a little phonograph – it was one of those that had a paper tube inside it that the music came out of when it was played. He was Indian but he had curly hair, so I think he was also part Russian.[13] Joluk had only one son and one daughter. Mom and I used to walk over there to visit. His wife was a friend of Mom's. She was from the Old Iliamna Village – her name was Nastashia.[14] Sometimes they would come over and visit us for a couple days. We enjoyed visiting with them.

Their only son drowned in Zip Creek up by the Old Iliamna Village. They sent Paul and Zenia Zachar 's Dad, Wanka[15] over to Pile River to tell them that their son died. Wanka was drunk and hollering and half crying. He shot the gun three times (this was the signal that someone had died), Joluk and his wife thought he was crazy and going to kill them. They ran away into the woods. But they came back and then Wanka told them the terrible news.

When Joluk moved to Pedro Bay, I don't know where they lived. He and his wife lived mostly in a tent. I think they might have stayed in that cabin by Sam Foss.[16] We liked to tease Joluk. We would go over to Knutsen Bay and sneak up on Joluk in his tent. He had a tent over there in Knutsen Bay. We would hear him talking to his wife then we would hit the roof pole just to startle him. He would laugh.

I know he cut wood for Sam Foss. He would cut about a cord for him and Sam would pay him, you know give him food and stuff he needed. Joluk would work for him.

He died in Eagle Bay, his heart quit on him while he was sleeping. I think that was where they buried him. He was down there with my brother Mike Jensen. They were living in a house right on the beach. Mike was living down there when he was doing the mail run. Joluk was with him, helping him out. His wife, Nastashia, had died.

People use the name of Joluk now as a joke or to say someone was lazy. I don't know why but people also called him 'Sixbits'. They also called him juicy mouth-the Indian word for that. I just remember that he made his money trapping and working for others.

Oh, when he was a young man he was a good runner. They would have him run letters over to Iliamna Bay. He would run all the way over and back in one day. Yeah, he was a mail messenger when he was young.

Old Juluk was our 'aida' – a friend, a good friend that you could have a lot of fun with - your 'aida'. You could talk about everything with him. Joluk was pretty good. He liked to tease us too, you know. Yeah, he was a nice old man. I liked Joluk.

Schooling

No, I never went to school – they closed the school before I was old enough to go.[17] My brothers: Mike, Nicolai, Gust and the other older kids like Fred Roehl went to school and knew how to read and do math. My sisters, Alma and Virginia both went to school, too. Yeah, Virginia got me started with the reading. I think I was around 10 when I started to learn to read.

I would just go to the old school building where they left everything and dig through the books, take whatever I wanted. I would take books with me when I went camping and trapping and study in the evenings. Yeah, I taught myself mostly and just learned along the way.

My mom didn't read. She wouldn't even speak English. She didn't even want to hear me talk in English. I only talked Indian with her. My brothers didn't speak Indian very well because they went to school where they had to speak only English and also they spent so much time away from home, away from my Mom. I learned English from them. I would have to interpret for them sometimes with Mom.[18]

On Building A House

All the houses were built by hand using axe and saw. They made the flooring out of cottonwood. It is easier to hew to make smooth. When you washed the cottonwood floor it would get nice and white. After the cottonwood floor boards dried out they shrunk. There would be cracks in the floor. They built the houses close to the ground so they didn't get cold in the winter. Then they would bank it up around the outside of the house with dirt and turf. This kept the cold air from getting in under the house.

They used tarpaper over the logs on the roof. Before they had tar paper they used skinny cottonwood poles to make a waterproof roof. They split those poles in half lengthwise, then hollowed each half out - two of them. They would place these two side by side on the roof with the hollowed out sides face up. Then they would split and hollow out another log that would go on top the two already there. This would go over the two below, you know face down and it wouldn't leak, it overlapped. This worked very well.

Old Iliamna School and teacher housing.

(NPS. Lake Clark National Park & Preserve. LACL H-488. Donated by Marie Millett, 1997)

Reindeer Herder in front of Old Iliamna Village School in 1908-09.

Breece said these young men were her special students when she taught at Old Iliamna Village School. They would travel about 40 miles up the lake and attend school for two weeks at a time.

There was a small house by the school for them to live in.

(Courtesy NPS. Lake Clark National Park & Preserve. LACL H-523. Donated by Ray Schlaben in 1994)

This is a good illustration of the kind of roof Walter describes. Photo taken between 1910-1912.

(Courtesy NPS. Lake Clark National Park & Preserve. LACL H-1851. Donated by Joanne Wolverton, 2002)

Gertrude Millett, daughter of Hugh and Maria (Roehl) Millett, sitting in potato garden in Old Iliamna Village.

(Courtesy NPS. Lake Clark National Park & Preserve. LACL H-562. Donated by Marie Millett in 1997.)

Two men whip sawing lumber at Foss Landing on Iliamna River circa May 1910. Charles Mcneil on top.

(NPS. Lake Clark National Park & Preserve. LACL H-1856.)

I remember that everybody had gardens. They were all fenced in so the dogs wouldn't get in to them. They grew potatoes, turnips, and rutabagas. I know as kids we would go into the garden to look for something to eat.[19]

Most people had cellars where they saved their old potatoes for seed potatoes. It was necessary to have a cellar because you couldn't keep the fire going all night and the house would freeze. They kept everything that they didn't want to freeze in the cellar.

Most of the houses had one bedroom and then a large main room that was used for kitchen, living and eating. The big house in the pictures of the Old Iliamna Village is my brother Grasim's. I don't know what happened to that house. He may have hauled it away. I don't remember what happened to any of the houses. After they closed the school, people just moved out, guess they took their houses with them.

Poisoned

My wife Annie's brother, Michael C Rickteroff, was poisoned in 1930.[20] He was traveling with Holly Foss from Bristol Bay on Holly's boat, *The Iliamna*. They had some groceries that they got from down there. I don't know for sure but I think it was sardines. Anyway, they were eating it one day and didn't finish it. So they just put it on the shelf. There was no refrigeration then, you know. The next day Michael C ate that open can of sardines. It killed him. He got sick and died before they made it back to the

Old Iliamna Village. Michael C's wife was Katherine Simeon. They were the parents of David Victoroff and Jenny Runstetler.[21] Yeah, I always think of Michael C whenever I eat sardines.

On My Brother Mike Jensen and His Mail Run

Mike Jensen was another brother of mine. He was born in 1906 or 1907, so he was about 15 years older than me. He was the oldest of Charlie Jensen's sons.[22] Mike's first wife was Elizabeth Rickteroff, daughter of Cusma and Mariia. Well, she wasn't Cusma's daughter, but like his ward. I think he and Mariia just raised her. I don't know who her parents were.[23]

This is Homoska Zachar, Michael A Rickteroff, and Charlie Jensen down by Charlie's place on the Kvichak River.

(Photo courtesy Mary Jensen.)

Mike and Elizabeth had two children, Carl and Freda Jensen.

Elizabeth died so then Mike married Katherine. Katherine was the daughter of Simeon Nikita and a woman named Yavdagia, also called Mrs. Simi. Katherine was the widow of Michael C Rickteroff. He is the guy that died from food poisoning. Mike and Katherine had two children, Mike and Albert Jensen.

I was pretty young when I would go with my brother Mike on his mail run. The mail would come across Cook Inlet from Seldovia on a barge to Iliamna Bay and then get hauled over the portage to Old Iliamna Village. Mike hauled the mail on his boat from Iliamna River down to the new village of Iliamna. Then he started going to Igiugig after they got a post office. Kokhanok was there but they didn't have a post office so he never went there. He made the trip once a month. It was fun, like riding on a big ferry or something. Most of the time Mike was by himself. Joluk helped him sometimes, too.

After Grasim died Mike got his boat, *The Advance*. He used it to do the mail run. He went down to Iliamna with mail one day. It was a beautiful calm day. The Seversens

Walter's brother, Mike Jensen on his mail boat in front of Lonesome Bay.
Walter said you can see that he is already sick with TB here.

(Photo courtesy Walter Johnson)

invited him over to their place for the night. He put a stock anchor on *The Advance*. These anchors weren't good for the hard lake floor, we used them down Bristol Bay. Well, he anchored it up by Slop Bucket Lake there in front of that big gravel beach. That night the east wind hit. He woke up and it was blowing east wind. So he went over to where he had anchored *The Advance*. It was too late. The boat was already on the shore and getting broken up by the waves.[24]

So he got another boat, I think it was a Bristol Bay boat. He built a cabin on it and put an engine in it. Mike was a pretty good carpenter. This boat was called the *Don't Worry*.

The last year that Mike did the mail run he was living down the Lake. First he was at Eagle Bay. This is where Joluk stayed with him to help him. Joluk's wife had died while they were at Pedro Bay. Mike had a house right on the beach there at Eagle Bay. The other houses in Eagle Bay were way up on the side of the mountain. Pete Sours and Donkoo Karlshekoff both lived there. There was like a little Indian village there at Eagle Bay. They had a creek that went right by their houses. But, yeah

Mike Jensen's boat at Sam Foss's dock in Pedro Bay, 1945. Mary thought that this was his last trip before he died.

(Photo courtesy Mary Jensen)

they lived way up the hill there. I think their houses were at least a mile above the water line.

After Joluk died Mike moved to Goose Bay. He moved into Aunt Valun's house. You know she and Charlie Roehl lived there for a while. Their house was in pretty good shape, so he moved into that.

He got TB while he was doing the mail run. Annie Kay Karlshekof was his wife at the time. Annie was the sister of Ephaim Karlshekoff, Donkoo's son. My Brother Mike died there in Goose Bay. They buried him in Pedro Bay. Mike and Annie had one son, Chris Jensen. Annie Kay moved up to Pedro Bay for a while, but it didn't work out for her there so she moved to Nondalton.

"Auntie Over"

We often played 'Auntie Over' on Annie's house. This would be her dad, Dick Mysee's house there in Old Iliamna Village. It had the best roof. You needed to be able to run all the way around the house, you know, chasing each other. This house was good for

Wasalisa Mysee in front of her newly built house in Old Iliamna Village.

(Photo courtesy of Walter Johnson)

that. You used a small rubber ball that you threw over the roof. The kids on the other side of the house had to catch it. If they caught it then they would come around and chase you trying to hit you with the ball. If you got hit you had to go on their side. The side that ended up with the most kids won. Yeah, we played that a lot.

Dick's house was big inside, so they had all the dances there, too. His house was the newest and biggest house in the Old Iliamna Village when I was young.

Summers at Tommy Point

My brothers Grasim and Nicolai would drop Mom and I off at Tommy Point on their way to Bristol Bay. They would help us get set up there for the summer then go on down to Bristol Bay to commercial fish. We would fish all summer there at Tommy Point, you know, catch salmon and smoke them. My

Aerial view of Tommy Point in spring. You can see the lake is still frozen. You can also see the buildings at the end of the isthmus that goes out to the island.

(Photo courtesy of Walter Johnson)

Mom was quite a worker. We had a really good smokehouse there.

Quite a few other people spent their summer in Tommy Point, too. My sister Alma would be there with us. She was already married and so Gillie would set her up in her own tent. There was a little house there that Mom and I stayed in.

Old Alec Flymn set his family up further up the beach by that spit that went across to the island. My brother Mike would bring his wife Elizabeth there, too. He had Carl and Freda then. They would live in a tent.

There was an old Man who would live there at Tommy Point in the summers, too. His name was Alushka. Did you hear this story? *"You know there was this man that discovered Alaska. When the man landed on the shore Alushka was there on the beach to greet him. This man asked him what his name was. He said 'Alushka', so that was what they called the place. Alaska."* [25]

Alushka was an old Indian from Old Iliamna Village. He came to Tommy Point every summer with us. During the winter he chopped wood for the school at Old Iliamna Village. He packed it all in from the woods on his back. I don't remember if he had a wife. He must have stayed with somebody, because I don't remember him having a house of his own in Old Iliamna Village.

After we stopped putting up fish in Tommy Point, everyone else quit, too. I think we did it for four or five years. I don't know why we stopped going there. I guess it just became easier to do the fish at home. You know, right there at Lonesome Bay.

Salmon harvest in Tommy Pt.

(Photo courtesy of Walter Johnson)

On Airplanes Landing in the Old Iliamna Village

Russell Merrill[26] was the first guy to land a plane on the river there at Old Iliamna Village. He was flying for McGee Airways. He died in Merrill Pass, you know. Well, he didn't actually land on the river. He landed down at the mouth of the river then I think it was Sam Foss who towed him up to the village. Yeah, it was pretty exciting for the people when he landed there in the Old Iliamna Village. This was in 1927.

The second guy I remember coming to the village was Jack Elliot. He came out of Anchorage, too. I think he flew for Star Airlines. Well, when he came to the village he gave people rides. I don't remember what he charged but he would fly them up to the mouth of the Iliamna River over to Pile Bay and back. He did that for quite a while then he flew back to Anchorage. I didn't go. I think this was in 1935 when I was 13.

A Murder and a Suicide

Ignatia Delkettie's mom was shot and killed by a white man named Hen Moore. This guy drank a lot. He shot her because the people of the village wouldn't let her live with

First airplane in front of Old Iliamna Village. The plane actually landed down at the mouth of the river and then was towed up to the village by Sam Foss.

(Photo courtesy of Walter Johnson)

him anymore. He didn't want to give her up. He shot her while she was out walking. Then he went back to his house and shot himself.

I don't know if Hen Moore was Ignatia's dad. Mom said that Ignatia was like an orphan. She said she would often ask him into her house so he could warm up and have something to eat. I don't know who was taking care of him after his mom was killed, my mom never told me that.[27]

Cemetery of Old Iliamna Village.

(NPS. Lake Clark National Park & Preserve. LACL H-645. Donated by Jane Jacobs in 1998.)

Russian Orthodox Church rebuilt in Pedro Bay.

(Photo courtesy of Walter Johnson.)

Oh, they wouldn't bury that guy in the cemetery with everyone else because of what he did. He was buried in an unmarked grave on the other side of the dog team trail. There was a very nice wide dog team trail that went by the cemetery. It went over to Pile Bay. This trail was like a road it was used so much for wood hauling. Anyway, they buried Hen Moore upside down all by himself. You know, they put him face down in his grave. Yeah, they put him there because of what he did.

Moving the Russian Orthodox Church

I remember when they moved the Russian Orthodox Church from Old Iliamna Village to Pedro Bay. Ignasia Delkettie was a lot of help moving the church. He came and lived in the Old Village that spring so he could help with the church. I remember Ignasia used dogs to drag the logs down to the beach. This was easier than packing them, because you know how the church was way up on the hill. It was a long ways down to the beach. It was spring so there was no ice in the river or on the lake. I think they floated all those logs down to Pedro Bay in a big raft. They tied all the logs together. I was a teenager then so I helped some with moving those logs.

Wanka Zachar built that church there in the Old Village. He was from Kenai and he built it just like the church that he saw over there at Kenai. He was a good carpenter. That church had those real nice notched corners. He helped with the rebuilding of it in Pedro Bay, too.[28]

A Raid and a Rout

A Distant Memory

"One time there were these two Indians living up on Iliamna River. They were both married. Well, one day they decided to go up the river to hunt. While they were up there something happened. Some Aleuts were traveling around the lake. These Aleuts weren't from the lower part of the lake. It was thought that they portaged over from the inlet side to where Kokhanak Bay is now. Anyway, it was quite a group of them. They came up the Iliamna River to where these Indians had their homes. They raided their homes and took their wives. A son got away and ran all the way up the river to find his Dad and told them what happened. The two Indians went back to their place and sure enough they could see what happened. Their wives were gone. They decided to go look for them. They headed down the river *and somehow had an idea of where the Aleuts would be. They went over to Pile River and sure enough they were there. These Aleuts were all sleeping. They had these big skin boats and they turned them upside down to sleep under. They made a nice shelter. Well, they called in Indian to their wives and told them to stay where they were. Then they yelled at the Aleuts and woke them all up. But each time an Aleut tried to come out from under the boats the two Indians would club them and kill them. Well, they did that until nearly all the Aleut men were dead. There were some old men left. They told them to go back to where they came from and never come back. The didn't kill them, but put them in their boats and pushed them off and told them to never come back."*

Walter's Mom, Anna Rickteroff Johnson. This was taken sometime in the 1920s.

(Photo courtesy of Mary Jensen)

Walter, On His Own

Losing Mom

Ignasia Delkettie, Virgil Delkettie's dad used to always come up to visit us in Lonesome Bay in the late fall. He was from the Old Iliamna Village but he married someone from Nondalton and moved there. He was related to us, but I can't remember how. Well, he was there in Lonesome Bay when Mom died in the fall of 1937. When someone dies you take a high-powered rifle and shoot it three times. That was what people did whenever someone died.

When Mom died, Grasim and his wife Sophie were there. Nicolai was there, too. He was married to Annie John at this time. Gillie and Alma were still there, too. Ignasia and I went over to the Old Iliamna Village to tell the people that my mom died.

We buried her in the Old Iliamna Village cemetery.

Mom had been sick for a while. Yeah, she was sick. They had taken her to Dillingham but there was nothing they could do for her. She had TB.

When Mom died I was only 15 years old, so I was on my own then. Oh, I had my older brothers. They were always around but still, I felt pretty much on my own. I felt that all I needed were a good pair of pants and some good shoepacks for my feet and I would be set.

Never Knew My Dad

After the memory from Copper River, I never saw my dad, Alf, again until I was 16 years old. Buck and I liked to play guitar in the bunkhouse when we were down in Bristol Bay. One day while we were playing guitar this guy walked in and he asked us where we were from. We didn't know who he was. I didn't know he was my dad. He asked, "Where are you boys from?"

We said we were from Old Iliamna Village. "Oh," he said. "What are your names?" I said we were Drafim Delkettie and Walter Johnson. "Gee," he said. "You must be my son." He had to leave right away because of the tide. He was in a hurry. He told us he had to leave, he was heading back to his place on Branch River and he had to catch the tide.

I saw him one more time after that. This was after I was married to Annie. I was 24 years old then. I had gone down to Bristol Bay with Sam Foss. Sam towed a sailing fish boat down there. Bennie Foss and Alice, Buck's sister, were on that boat.

My Dad, Alf, was fishing for Red Salmon Cannery down below Naknek. I fished there that summer on Bennie Foss's boat.

We were headed back up to Lake Iliamna and Sam Foss had that sailboat in tow. My dad just happened to be waiting for a ride to go up to Levelock. So I told him, "Why don't you ride with us in the sailboat?" He did. I had a ride with my dad for about three hours on that trip to Levelock, but we didn't talk about anything. I don't think we talked at all. Then we dropped him off at Levelock and traveled on up the Kvichak River to Lake Iliamna. That was the last time I saw him.

Yeah, he always lived there on Branch River but I never saw him. He never remarried. Lived all alone on that river until he died. I guess he was a good friend of Guy Groat. Guy spent a lot of time visiting him there on Branch River.

He was a stranger to me. I didn't know him. He was born in Estonia. But he came here from New York. He came with quite a group of white men.

There were quite a few white people in Old Iliamna Village a long time ago. My mom would tell me about them sometimes.

She didn't like to go over to the village because there was so much drinking and bad stuff going on over there when those guys were all living there in the Old Village.[1]

Yeah, all I knew about my dad was that he was born in Estonia and grew up in New York City. Never knew my dad.[2]

Living in Lonesome Bay

After Dad left us there in Lonesome Bay in 1927, Grasim built himself a house there so there were two houses for several years. Then Mike Jensen, my other brother built a house but he didn't stay very long. He moved back to old Iliamna Village then down to Jack Durand's.

Gillie and Alma were the next ones to build there. Alma was in her twenties when she married Gillie Jacko. One winter my brothers, Nicolai and Mike went beaver trapping up the Chulitna River. Alma went with them. That's where they met Gillie Jacko. Gillie was from Stoney River area. But at this time he was living in Nondalton with his grandparents. Gillie Jacko and my sister, Alma lived in Lonesome Bay a long time, most of their kids were born there. They were the only ones there that had a garden. Well they moved to Pedro Bay. Gillie and Alma were like the second family to move to Pedro Bay after Sam and Sophie Foss settled there.

My uncle, William Mike Rickteroff, Mom's brother, moved to Lonesome Bay from Goose Bay in 1932. He moved into Mike's old house. He was still married to Annie John and they had three kids: James, Mary and William.

William Mike liked to drink. He would chop wood for days, every day he would chop wood until he had a pretty big pile. That's when I would help him. I didn't like to because he was such a slow man. He did everything in a slow way and I would get impatient. Well, after he had a good pile of wood he would open up his bivak (home brew) barrel and get drunk. He would be drunk for about a week.

He died when I was around twelve, about two years after he moved to Lonesome Bay. His wife Annie married my brother Nicolai, she died about a year after that. William Mike and Annie's kids were still pretty young. William went to his Mom's relatives in Kokhanak. Mary stayed for a while with Gillie and Alma then went up to Pedro Bay and stayed with Sam and Sophie. James stayed in Lonesome Bay.

After Mom died one of my brothers Gust Jensen and a cousin, Buck Delkettie, came over to Lonesome Bay and lived with me the rest of that winter. Gust was 20 years old and Buck was 16. Buck was sort of an orphan so he spent a lot of time with us at Lonesome Bay.

Walter's brother, Gust Jensen in his army uniform.

(Photo courtesy Mary Jensen)

Gust was five years older than me. His Dad was a John Pedersen. I didn't know him. He got sick and had to leave, he died so he never got to come back. Gust wasn't around much. He lived mostly in the Old Iliamna Village with one of our older brothers so he could attend school.

Buck's mom was Mary, my mom's younger sister.[3] She died when Buck was 13. His Dad's name was Gallela Delkettie and he died about a year after his wife Mary. I remember when he died. Buck and I were down at Scow Bend, someone loaned us an outboard motor and we were at Scow Bend chopping wood when we heard the three shots. We knew it was Gallela. He had been sick for a long time. They thought it was pneumonia. Buck didn't like his brother-in-law, his older sister Mary's husband, so he lived with us mostly. Yeah, he was 16 when he came to live with us. He was like a brother.

Frank Rickteroff was about my age, too.[4] He would often come over and stay with us. Yeah, he was around a lot. His Dad was Evon Rickteroff. Lillian and Lolla were his sisters. You know, Lolla married my brother Nicolai after his first wife, Annie died.

My brothers, Nicolai and Gust Jensen, my cousin, Buck Delkettie and a friend, Pete Nagin were all called to go into the army three years after Mom died. Pete had lived with us for several years there in Lonesome Bay, with my brothers and me. We knew him from Bristol Bay. One summer he didn't make enough money to get back to his home on Afognak Island. So we told him to come home with us. We were traveling on Mike's old boat *The Don't Worry*. It was in pretty bad shape but we made it up to Lonesome Bay. Well, Pete ended up staying with us for a couple years. Yeah, they were all called into the army. I was left behind because I was too young at that time. I did register later, when I turned 18, but they never did call for me.

Walter drew this to show how he remembers Lonesome Bay when he lived there. FROM LEFT TO RIGHT – cache, smokehouse, brother Grasim's house, Gillie and Alma Jacko's house, Walter's house, and the house his brother Mike Jensen built.

Oh yeah, Nicolai came back. They wouldn't take him into the army. I don't know why they wouldn't take him, but I guess he had something wrong with him. Anyway, he came back to Lonesome Bay.

I lived alone after they left for the army, after Mom died. It was pretty lonely. Gillie and Alma were there, so were Grasim and Nicolai but I was alone in the house. Yeah, I was 17 years old and living alone. It was quiet after everyone left.

I lived in Lonesome Bay until I got married at the age of 24 in 1946. Yeah, Gust got married a year before me and he moved to Pedro Bay. This was after he got out of the army. He married Mary Balluta.[5] He and Mary lived with her Great Grandma, Mrs. Sinkga[6] for a couple years until he built his own house above the small sand beach.

Once, when I was alone in Lonesome Bay, I heard an airplane. It was a dark night. I took the gas lamp and put it against the window then took it away. I kept doing that and then all of a sudden a big light came down from the plane and shone on my house. I didn't do that anymore, but I know it wasn't the Japanese.[7]

I think Nicolai was the last one to live up there at Lonesome Bay. That was the fall of 1948.[8]

On Making Money

Most of our money we made by commercial fishing in Bristol Bay. But in the winter we made some money by trapping. Sometimes there would be odd jobs, too. Like when we worked on a trails project. This project was building a trail from Lonesome Bay to Pedro Bay. Sam Foss got money from the government to have a trail cut

Boat full of fish tail harvest.

(NPS. Lake Clark National Park & Preserve. LACL H-560. Donated by Marie Millett in 1997)

Head of Iliamna Bay, also called Williamsport. These warehouses belonged to Fred Roehl, Sr. Trucks also belonged to him.

(NPS. Lake Clark National Park & Preserve. LACL H-583)

Holly Foss with his barge, a truck and a tracked vehicle at Foss's Landing.

(NPS. Lake Clark National Park & Preserve. LACL H-588. Donated by Helena Seversen Moses in 1992)

out. We didn't make very much. I worked and only made about five dollars a day. I think I was only 15 or 16 years old. We cut a portage all the way to Pile River. It was a much better trail for driving dog teams on after we cut it out. In some places we put down logs, over the swampy places, you know. From Pedro Bay it went up to Dumbbell Lakes and down through Chayi Camp. That was a pretty steep section of the trail. Once you made it down that part of the trail you wanted to stop for a cup of chayi, you know, tea.

Another way to make money was to sell trout tails. Yeah, everyone was catching trout for the tails to sell them because there was a bounty on trout. I would sell them and use that money to get what I needed. We'd send our trout tails down to Iliamna and Hobson, Steve and May's Dad, bought them and counted them then destroyed them. Hans Seversen used to buy them for five dollars a hundred. That's why Annie and her folks did a lot of fishing. They made a lot of money selling trout tails.[9]

Seversen bought our furs, too.[10] He had to ship his fur out to Seattle. He had a place in Iliamna Bay, a big place full of furs. He would hire someone to watch or guard it for him until the freight boat came from Seldovia to take the furs out.

Freight over the Portage

The furs were hauled from the Old Iliamna Village over the portage to Iliamna Bay either by walking and packing or with dog team. Summit Pass was pretty steep. You dropped off the top of Summit Pass just like you are going to drop

The Iliamna in dry dock. This is the boat Holly freighted in.
(Photo courtesy Walter Johnson)

Holly Foss & Hans Seversen at Foss's Landing with a pile of freight ready to be loaded onto the barge. You can see most things are in wooden crates. A third person with back turned unidentified.

(NPS Lake Clark National Park & Preserve. LACL H-283. Donated by Helena Seversen Moses in 1992.)

This is either Evon Rickteroff or Dick Micey with horses loaded with freight. They look to be on their way to Foss's landing. This is sometime in the 1920s.

(NPS. Lake Clark National Park & Preserve. LACL H-958. Donated by Matt & Mary Davey, 1997.)

off a steep cliff. It was pretty hard with a dog team. First, you would unhitch the dogs from the sled, take them down the drop-off one by one, and tie them up to the willows below. Then you would very carefully take your sled down. You had to put two braces on the runners so it wouldn't slide so fast.

Going up that was pretty tough, too. You had to get your dogs up by leading them. They would be scared, too. But they even got eggs that came in big boxes over that portage.

All the freight was stacked on the bank by Old Foss's place. That is where they stacked all the freight that they hauled from Iliamna Bay. This was before the road went to Pile Bay. It ended right there by Foss's place. Yeah, all that freight was piled up there at Foss's Landing and covered with tarp so it wouldn't get wet. Getting the stuff there was pretty tough. Sometimes there was no snow over the portage, bare ground. When that happened you just had to pack it all.

Someone would then freight it down the lake. Different guys did that. Alex Flymn, Jr. did for a while before he moved to Homer and freighted between Homer and Iliamna Bay. Hans Seversen ran that boat, *The Tern*. Holly Foss did it too. His boat was called *The Iliamna*.

Drinking

One day when I was about 16 years old, Frank Rickteroff and I were over at the Old Village. I think we were the only young teenage boys in the village at that time. Well, the older men wanted us to drink like them, you know, out in the open. This was their way. You know they didn't want the young people to sneak with drinking or smoking.

Evon Rickteroff with his wife Stepenita, daughter, Lolla (seated). Woman in white cap unknown.

(NPS. Lake National Park & Preserve. LACL H-707. Donated by Bert & Edna Foss, 1995)

I guess they thought 16 years of age was old enough. Anyway, they told us, "We want you and Frank to be down at Evon's house." This was Evon Rickteroff, Frank's Dad.[11] So we went down to Evon's house.

They put a big pot of bivak (home brew) on the table.[12] Told us both to sit down at the table. They didn't give us tea or coffee or anything. They just had the home brew and cigarettes on the table before us. They told us to drink the bivak and smoke the cigarette. They said, "You do this then you will be alright. You won't be stealing or sneaking. You do it in front of us, anytime you want." So, I took the cigarette. I smoked my cigarette. I had already been smoking. They poured the bivak in a big cup and put it in front of us. Frank drank his, he really wanted to drink, you know. He had already started. But, I wouldn't touch it. They asked me why I wouldn't drink. I said I didn't like it. I didn't want to drink that stuff. So they let me go – they didn't try to force me. But, yeah that was their way of getting the young guys to know that they didn't have to sneak or steal the stuff if they wanted it.

I think most of the men in the village drank, even all my brothers. They would go on binges and be drunk for a week at a time. Most would have a big barrel going in their house. After they had been drunk for a week or so then they would be okay for a long time. But I can't remember any man in the village that didn't get drunk.

It used to make me so mad when they would drink. Sometimes they would order wine through Ed McKinnet, you know he handled the freight at Iliamna Bay. When they got their wine they would be drunk for a long time on that. Later when Art Lee started his business down there in Iliamna they would order liquor from him. Boy, that was bad stuff.

That was why I would go out into the woods camping by myself so much. I just wanted to get away from that drinking, because it just made me so mad. I would just put on my backpack and take off, be gone for days.

On Play

We did a lot of skiing, Buck Delkettie and I. We had regular cross-country skis that we ordered from the Sears catalog. We would ski to Pile River and back. Sometimes we would go up to Lonesome Bay Mountain – take us about four hours to get up there and then ski down. That was fun. We wouldn't be able to see very well because it would be so bright and white with the sun shining on the snow. We would make our own jumps. Skiing was real fun.

One winter a couple guys came over the road and camped up above the bridge for about a month. They had skies and they skied all over, that is some pretty rough and brushy country they were skiing in. Once we tried to follow them – we wanted to see how they skied. We didn't know who they were or why they were there. This must have been 1938 or '39.

We had bicycles, too. We would ride over to Iliamna Bay on the road. We had to carry our bicycles over to the road from Lonesome Bay, so we could bike there. We were in our teens then.

Sometimes we would just hike over the road to see how fast we could walk the road from Foss's place. The fastest we did it was three hours. It is about 10 miles from the Foss place there across the river from Old Iliamna Village to Iliamna Bay.

We also did a lot of ice-skating when the lake was good for that. We used those old tie-on skates. I don't know where we got our skates from, but most everyone had some.

Most people skated. I remember Gillie Jacko was a good skater. Some people had the shoe kind, but I liked the tie-ons better because they didn't hurt my feet so much.

On Boats

The first boat I owned was an old double ender sailboat. I bought it at Koggiung. I went there and asked if I could buy one of the old unused boats that were sitting there in the yard. The foreman told me to go ahead and pick one out. I looked them over and picked out a good one. Paid $75 for that boat. I was 19 at the time. Sailed it up the Kvichak, most of the way. My brother Mike had his boat with an inboard engine, I think it was the *Don't Worry.* Anyway, when there wasn't any wind or going against the current was hard he would tow me. I kept that boat for three years. It was good for traveling around on the Lake.

This is the type of boat Walter used to sail around the lake.

(Photo courtesy of Walter Johnson)

I fished it, too. It was pretty small. I would put 2500 fish in it and boy it would be loaded!

One fall day in 1942 my brother Mike invited Nicolai and Gillie to go over to Jack Durand's where he was living at that time for his birthday. Well, they were already drunk when they left, Nicolai and Gillie. There was a terrible east wind. It was coming out of Pile Bay like crazy. The water looked like snow flying when the wind picked it off the lake. Well, they headed out of Lonesome Bay and then their motor quit on them. I watched them for a while then told James Rickteroff to go with me in my sailboat. It looked like they needed help. Well, by the time we got to them they had gotten their engine going and headed on for Jack Durand's. I kept going, too. We only had up a half sail – I don't think we could have made it with both sails up. The wind was pretty strong and I didn't think I would be able to make it back to Lonesome Bay in one tack. Well, we beat Nicolai and Gillie over to my brother's place, and they had an engine, an outboard. We pulled into that bay just on the east side of Jack Durand's. It

Virginia Jensen, Dolly Foss, Nicolai Karshekoff sitting on logs in front of Foss home in Pedro Bay.

These logs were to be used to build an addition onto the Foss home.

(Photo courtesy of Dolly Foss Jacko)

was nice and calm there. That was where we spent the night. Didn't want to go over to my brother's because they were drinking. I didn't like that. I didn't like to be around them when they went crazy with that stuff. Yeah, that sailboat was pretty good. Next morning we got up and sailed back to Lonesome Bay.

In 1944 I traded it for a 16-foot boat with a Nine HP Johnson outboard motor. This boat used to belong to Trygve Olsen, Annie's first husband. I think he built it. It was made with real narrow boards, shiplap. It was a pretty nice boat. Frank Rickteroff bought it from him so I traded with Frank to get it. Having an engine was pretty nice. It was sure a lot easier to get around on the lake with an outboard motor. There weren't many of those motorboats around at that time. It was nicer than the sailboat for traveling around, especially going from Lonesome Bay to Pedro Bay. The boat was called the *Hornet*. This was why I named my fishing boat the *Hornet*.

On My Sister – Virginia

Virginia was another sister, younger than Alma.[13] We all had the same Mom but different Dads. Alma and Virginia's Dad was Charlie Jensen.[14]

Virginia's first husband was Chester Horton. He was a friend of my brothers, Mike and Nicolai. They were good friends with him when they trapped in Kaskanak for a couple winters. They got to know him there. He just got sick one day and died, I think he had a stroke. This was about a year after he and Virginia were married.

About a year later Virginia married Gory Nicolai, also called Gregory, the son of old Chudda Nicolai and Marfa Rykterov.[15] Chudda Nicolai's house was right above Annie's in Old Iliamna Village, you know her folk's house, Wasalisa and Dick Mysee. Chudda Nicolai was an old Indian. He burned up when his house burned down. It went so fast they couldn't get him out. I don't know where Gory lived after that. I know he spent a lot of time with the Roehls so maybe that was where he lived. Gory Nicolai and my sister, Virginia lived in Goose Bay their first year. I think Gory built a place down there. He was a good friend of the Roehl boys. After the fishing season of 1942 they came up to Lonesome Bay because they were going to spend that winter there.

That same fall I decided to go down to Squirrel Village to trap. I had my sailboat then. I wanted to go down to Squirrel Village because this was a pretty good place for mink. James Rickteroff was going with me. He was only 15 years old. I was 20.

Well, we got ready to go and Gory came down to the beach to see us off. He said, "I'll see you when you get back. If something happens to me, I'll let you know." Well, you know that was a funny thing to say, but I never thought anything about it. James and I left for Squirrel Village to do our trapping.

When we got to Squirrel Village we pulled the boat up and stayed there for 42 days. Never saw anyone else that whole time. One night after we had gone to bed I heard something walking around outside the tent. I thought maybe it was just a moose. I looked out but didn't see anything. I didn't think anything of it at the time.

One day I told James, "I'd like to take a walk up to Mike Jensen's place." Mike, my brother, was staying at Jack Durand's. You know that little bay up there. He built a house up there and Annie Kay Carlzekoff was his wife then. They had Carl then and Freda, but I don't think Carl was there. He was going to school someplace in Petersburg. We walked all the way up there, about 10 or 11 miles. It is quite a ways. I didn't want to take James, because he's crippled you know and couldn't walk very well. I could make it like nothing myself. I tried to make him stay but he wouldn't stay.

I said, "Okay, we'll walk." The lake was frozen over so we couldn't use the boat, but we couldn't use the ice either. We had gotten pretty close to Mike's place when James said he couldn't go anymore. We had about five more miles to go. I held his hand for a while but he got more tired. He told me, "Why don't you just keep on going to Mike's place and I will get there some time?" "No", I said, "I don't want to leave you out here by yourself. You don't know when a storm is going to come up. I will carry you." So, I put him on my back and I carried him. I carried him until I was pretty tired. He was pretty heavy and I got too tired to carry him any further. So I put him down again and let him walk. We didn't have very far to go, but it was getting dark. Finally, it did get dark and we

Gus Jensen and Gory Nicolai
(Photo courtesy of Walter Johnson)

were just on the other side of that point before Jack Durand's. There is that hill there you know. We had to make a portage over that hill. It was a pretty steep bank we had to get up and the deep snow made it very difficult. I had a pretty hard time getting him up there. I drug him and pulled him, but we made it and from there it was easy. We made it to my brother Mike's place.

Emilio Licalsi with Thelma Jacko and Victor Nicolai (Virginia's son).

(Photo courtesy of Walter Johnson.)

This is when Mike told me what happened to Gory. Gory, George, my nephew, and Nicolai, my brother, had gone up to the big lakes by Pile River, Goolu Lakes. There are two lakes up there, one was large and other was smaller and further up. They went up to the bigger Goolu Lake. They made a camp and Nicolai stayed in the camp. They went up there to set out traps, to look for game and tracks, you know. Gory and George went out. They were going to just walk up towards the little lake and check things out. It wasn't very long and George came running back. He said, " Gory was walking ahead of me and I was carrying my .22 rifle and holding the barrel and I don't know what happened. Something must have caught the trigger and the gun went off and shot Gory right in the back of the head."

Nicolai went to see and sure enough there was Gory lying there dead. He had been hit right in the back of the head. They weren't too far from Lonesome Bay. They went back to the camp because it was too late to do anything that day. Then the next day they went to Pedro Bay and told Sam Foss about it. Sam and several others went up there and looked it over and got Gory out. I don't know where they buried him. George was only about 10 years old when that happened. He is my sister Alma's son.

Well, that was when I thought about what Gory had said to me and how I had heard someone walking around outside our tent over there at Squirrel Village. I guess maybe he was letting me know that something had happened to him.

Virginia and Gory had a son, Victor Nicolai. Alma and Gillie Jacko took care of him.[16]

Virginia was married a third time after that to Emilio Licalsi. It didn't work out and he went back to the Lower 48. She never remarried but had another boy, Johnny Evan, who was adopted by Sam and Sophie Foss. Johnny's Dad was George Seversen, Hans Seversen's son. Virginia didn't do very well after that.

First Trip to Anchorage

In 1942 we had a really good fishing season. My brother, Nicolai, a friend, George Seversen and myself decided to go to Anchorage for a trip. George had lived for a time in the Old Iliamna Village with his Dad, Hans Seversen.[17]

Sam Foss, who was the Commissioner of the Lake Iliamna Area, told us to take Effim Karsekoff[18] with us and leave him in Anchorage. Effim was a problem in the village. He was always stealing or doing bad things and Sam wanted to be rid of him.

Effim, Joluk's grandson, was five years younger than me. His mom was Martha. I was 20 years old at this time, so he would have been 15 years old. Anyway, we ended up taking Effim along and paying for his food and lodging there in Anchorage. It was okay because we had plenty of money from fishing. But we felt sorry for him and just couldn't leave him there by himself so we brought him back to the Old Iliamna Village with us. He didn't have anyplace to stay there in Anchorage, you know, and we couldn't just leave him.

Well, the hotel was cheap. I think it was the Morrison Hotel. We only paid fifty cents a night. It was cheap because there was no view. It just looked out at another building. Nicolai got a nicer room that looked down on the street. He paid a dollar a night for that room. We enjoyed looking out at the people on the street.

We took the boat *Princess Pat* from Iliamna Bay. It stopped at Seldovia, Homer Spit, Kasilof, and then Anchorage. We stayed there in Anchorage for a month, because that was when the boat would take us back to Iliamna Bay. It was the same boat and it made the same stops on the way back. The trip was made once a month throughout the summer.

Frankie Zachar, Bennie Foss, Dolly Foss in Pedro Bay.

(Photo courtesy of Dolly Foss Jacko)

We had a good time there in Anchorage. We didn't do much but mostly wandered around to look at things. That was also the first time I saw Homer and liked it.

Effim (Epheme) Karshekoff

You know Effim ended up having a pretty hard time. People in Pedro Bay thought he killed Frankie Zachar, Homoshka's stepson. Frankie was just a teenager. They were out in the boat coming into Pedro Bay and Frankie fell overboard. Effim said he tried to save him but couldn't. I guess he was drinking so it is hard to know what really happened. I think this happened sometime in the 1940s.

Later he did kill a man in Anchorage. He said the guy kept giving him a bad time. Finally, he got really mad and started hitting this guy with a stick, he kept hitting him and ended up killing him. He was drinking then, too. Effim went to jail for that but they didn't keep him in there very long.

He got married later to a white lady there in Anchorage. Then he got cancer and died not too much later. Yeah, he had a hard life.

My Freighting Experience with the *Don't Worry*

Buck Delkettie got a hold of my brother Mike's boat, the *Don't Worry* after Mike passed away. Shortly after he got the boat, Buck had to go into the army. So he took the boat up to Airplane Slough on Iliamna River in front of the village and parked the boat there. The water raised, the river was bank full that year. The boat just sank there. You talk about a mess that boat was, the mud was everywhere. Well, I took it out of there after the water went down. I cleaned it up. What a mess it was. I was 18 years old when I did that. I rescued that old boat. It didn't look like it could be used but I took a chance and got all the water out of it. Took the engine out and cleaned it up. Put it back together and it worked pretty well. I had myself a boat. I corked up the sides where the cracks opened up. I had to put some boards between the ribs and then caulk it. If I didn't do that the cotton wouldn't stay, the cracks were so big. It leaked quite a bit. Had to pull it up whenever I stopped at a beach because it would swamp. We had block and tackle in the boat all the time so we could pull it up out of the water.

I freighted in that boat, the *Don't Worry*. I used it to haul freight from Pile Bay to Iliamna all the way into February – it was the year when they built the Iliamna airport. I think it was 1940, so I was 18 years old. I was hauling stuff for the Iliamna airport. I would take Frank Rickteroff along as my helper.

Then after the lake froze they hired me down there in Iliamna to work on the airport. The lake froze up in March. I just left the boat right there on the beach in Iliamna. It sank there. I stayed in Iliamna and worked. I quit when it was time to go fishing. My boss didn't want me to quit, but I had to go fishing.

A Skating Incident

One winter day when I was 20 years old I decided to skate down to Pedro Bay. The ice was good, so I skated down to Pedro Bay and spent the night. Frank Rickteroff was there and decided to join me. I wanted to skate over to Jack Dorand's on the other side of the Lake. We had these old skates that you tied onto your shoes. That was what we used to skate with. Outside of Jack Dorand's there is a place so deep that it never froze very well there, and the ice would get bad real quick in that spot. Well, the lake was frozen up and it looked good. The ice was about a foot thick, maybe less. We skated over to my brother Mike Jensen's place there at Jack Dorand's. Joluck and his wife were staying there, too. They were living in a tent. Mike wasn't there so we didn't stay long and headed on up the Lake to Old Iliamna Village. The ice was very smooth, great skating.

I was skating ahead of Frank. He was a slow person. He was skating a ways behind me. I was going along at a good pace when I saw what looked like new ice, fresh ice. I couldn't stop. I went right onto that new ice. It held me up for about 20 feet, then I broke through that thin ice and went down. Boy, I was going way down. I started to tread water and that slowed my downward movement.

Walter Johnson as a young man talking to Aggie O'Hara in front of his sister Alma's house in Pedro Bay.

(Photo courtesy Dolly Foss Jacko)

Frank looked up and didn't see me. He kept following my tracks then saw the hole where I went in. He said he could see me and I looked like I was way down there.

I finally came back up to the surface. I saw Frank just standing there. He was looking around. I guess he was looking for something to stick out to me. Finally, he started to untie his backpack. We used to tie our packs on us with hanging twine. He couldn't untie it so he just busted the string – have to be pretty strong to do that.

He threw me the strap of his pack. I grabbed a hold of it and he started to pull me. I could see he was pulling too fast. I saw that it was going to break, I told him to slow down, so he slacked off a bit. I got my legs out and he pulled me to the safe ice. Boy, it was cold. There was a cold west wind coming up the lake. We were about a mile out from Jack Dorand's and my brother Mike's cabin.

My hair was frozen and my clothes were frozen. So I started skating immediately. I had to skate as fast as I could. We went to the house. Mike still wasn't home, but his wife, Annie Kay was there. Carl, Mike's son, wasn't there but Freda, his daughter, was there. I asked Mike's wife for some dry clothes. She gave me some and I went over to old man Joluk's tent. Joluk had a tent. Yeah, he was living in a tent in the winter.

I changed my clothes, and put on those dry clothes. Then Frank and I took off again. We didn't stay there. Yeah, we went along the beach and skated up to the Old Iliamna Village. It had been a long day.

I stayed over a couple nights in Old Iliamna Village with Frank. I don't know why Frank was living up there in his dad's old house. There wasn't anyone else living there, everyone had moved away. So Frank was living there by himself that winter.

Well, I had a cut on my face and a black eye. I had a .22 pistol on my side, you know in the case. But, I don't think I had a knife. That was some day. Good thing I had Frank with me.

Alec Flymn, Jr. with his wife, Annie and sons Mike & Willie at their home near Kokhonak Bay just before house is moved. Photo taken by Dennie Moore in 1944.

(Photo courtesy of Walter Johnson.)

Buck and Jessie (Millett) Delkettie at Millet's Place.

(Photo courtesy of Mary Jensen.)

Moving A House

Alec Flymn Jr. had built a house over by Hogh Bay. His dad lived further up in Kohkonak Bay.[19]

He built there because he grew up in the area and I guess to be close to his folks. Then he decided to move to Pile Bay. He was married to Annie. I think he met Annie at NN Cannery down the Bay, you know Bristol Bay. They had two sons, Mike and Willie.

Well, he cut his house into four parts to move it to Pile Bay. Pat Patterson, Alec's Dad and I were there to help. We were all there to help him move his house. After cutting it into four parts we carried it down to the beach and put it on the barge. It was the barge that Alec and Fred Roehl used to haul freight on the lake. I was about 22 years old at this time, so this must have been in the late summer of 1944. Boy, we didn't even break a window while moving that house. We got it to Pile Bay and put it back together, came out pretty good.

A Mining Job

Gust and I did a mining job. I am not sure how old I was but I think it was right after Gust got out of the army, you know, before he got married. This was in the fall after fishing.

This mining engineer by the name of Rutledge came to the lake. He wanted to check out Millett's site. You know the site where Hugh's dad worked. So Gust and I went and worked at Millett's old site for about a month.

The Milletts were long gone, so we moved into their old house. It was a long low house. That guy Rutledge was a pretty tall guy. Boy! He would keep hitting his head when he walked into the door. You know the house was pretty old and the roof was sagging down.

Well, we were looking for copper. We dug quite a few ditches. We would run into copper stains. It was kind of blue and like sand. What we found was copper. Well, we did that for just about a month.

Boy, Old Man Millett sure dug a big hole there.

The Boy They Didn't Get

A Distant Memory

I know another story about the 'invisible people'. It is also about my mom and Mrs. Joluk. My mom told me this story. Our people used to always go to the saltwater side from Old Iliamna Village. They would go over there in the early spring to get seafood. My mom was just a teenager and Mrs. Joluk was about the same age. I don't know who this boy was that they took along to help them get wood, but he was a cousin to them. My mom never told me his name. They had a skiff over there that they would use to go along the shoreline and pick dry wood off the beach. They called this place Qanlcha Nut'[1], it is way out where

Iliamna Bay ends. There was an island near it. They used to have a light on that island – a lighthouse. That was where they used to spend the summer. Most of the men were out hunting sea otters.

My mom and Mrs. Joluk rowed along the beach and they found some wood and this young guy was picking wood, too. But, he went further away from them and then he never came back. After they got lots of wood in the boat they waited for the young boy. They waited and waited. They hollered for him. He just wasn't around. So Mom told Mrs. Joluk, "Let's go look for him."

They followed his tracks where he went. There was a grassy bank. The grass on this grassy bank was all tramped down like a lot of people had walked on it. So they said, "Let's go up on this hill and look, see if he is up there."

That was where they found him, up on that grassy bank on a little ridge. They saw him lying flat on his face. So they started calling him and shaking him and he woke up. When he woke up he was so scared he wouldn't look around. He said he could still see those spirit people, the _____ that took him. He had no clothes on. The invisible people took all his clothes off and put them up on a tree. They had to climb the tree to get the clothes. They put his clothes on him. They had to hold him on each arm to help him back to the skiff because he was so weak and scared and wouldn't open his eyes. They put him in the bow of the boat. He said he wanted something to cover his head. They covered his head and took him back to their camp, to where they were living. Some of the people were just like priests, you know. They used to read the Bible in the church. Well, these people started reading the Bible to him. After they did that for a while, he finally got better. He woke up and he wasn't afraid anymore. So the _____ didn't get him.

Annie Mysee Olsen with son Trygve and daughter Ethel in front of her house in Pedro Bay. This is shortly before she married Walter.

(Photo courtesy of Dolly Foss Jacko)

Left Lonesome Bay

Getting Married

Annie and I were married on May 16, 1946. Sam Foss married us, he was the Commissioner, you know. Then we got married in the Russian Orthodox Church. I am not sure why, but I guess that was what was expected. She had been married before to Trygve Olsen.[2] She had two kids when I married her, Trygve and Ethel.

After I married Annie, I moved to Pedro Bay and we lived there in her house. She had her own house there in Pedro Bay. Sam Foss had it built for her. Her first husband left her after they were married for about two years. They were living down in Barney's Bay. That was too far for her to live alone. He, Trygve had bought all the materials to build a house but never got it built. So Sam had those materials moved and built for her right there in the village. We lived there in that house for four to five years. I then sold it to Carl and Hazel Jensen.

I was 24 years old when I married and finally left Lonesome Bay.

On Dick Mysee

Annie's father was Dick Mysee.[3] He was a good-looking guy. I don't know who his dad was. He liked wearing cool boots. From his pictures you can see he liked to dress up. He wasn't a lazy man. He was a good carver – he would always carve toys for the kids. No one knows who his parents were. When he was young folks would take him in to their homes to warm him up, especially in the winter and feed him. He always did like me.

Walter and Annie's sons Johnny and Howie
in Pedro Bay, winter of 1949.

(Photo courtesy of Walter Johnson.)

Pedro Bay children in the late 1940s. Billy Barber, Alvin Foss, Bert Foss, Trygve Olsen. Girl is Pauline Kolyaha.

(Photo courtesy Walter Johnson.)

Ahojik was Dick's real name, you know, his Indian name. Not much was known about him, just that he grew up in the Old Iliamna Village.

Dick Mysee wasn't Annie's real dad. Her real dad was Sophus Hendrickson.[4] Sophus was a Norwegian and a cousin of Sam and Hollie Foss. But Dick raised Annie like a dad.

Dick died down at Bristol Bay, at Nushagak. He is buried down there, because they couldn't get him back up to Pedro Bay.

Dick Mysee in Naknek, Late 1920s.

(NPS. Lake Clark National Paqrk & Preserve. LACL H-983. Donated by Agnes Cusma in 1998.)

On My Brother Nicolai Jensen, (1910-1947)

Nicolai was the second son of my mom and Charlie Jensen, born 1910, so he was 12 years older than me. He lived with us after my dad left us. Yeah, Nicolai helped us out through most of that time, after Dad left, you know, until he (Nicolai) got married.

When I was maybe 10 or 11, my uncle William Mike died. Nicolai married William Mike's widow, Annie. Nicolai and Annie had one child that died. Annie died soon after from TB. They weren't married for very long.

Annie's family came often to visit her. Once when it was blowing a pretty strong West wind her parents came in a bidarka. They were just surfing along on those big west wind rollers, coming into Lonesome Bay. They would come all the way from Kokhanok to Lonesome Bay in their bidarka to visit. I guess they would camp along the way. Annie's brothers would come, too. They had a sailboat and I think later they even had a boat with an engine. Yeah, they would come to visit. Boy, they would almost always be drunk when they came. They were young guys then – in their twenties. I think they were mixed blood. Annie was for sure – she didn't look like a full blood Eskimo.

Brothers Sam & Hollie Foss, with cousin Sophus Hendrickson, and Jack Webster in front of Old Iliamna Village, late 1920s.

(NPS. Lake Clark National Park & Preserve. LACL H-450. Donated by Marge Jensen.)

After my brother Grasim died and his wife Sophie moved away, Nicolai moved into their house. It was a better house than that old house of William Mike's. Shortly after moving into Grasim's house Nicolai married Lolla Rickteroff, Frank Rickteroff's half-sister. Boy, they weren't married even two years, I don't think, and then she died from T.B. too. There was a lot of T.B. those days.

Nicholai was alone then (not married) when he was shot. The kids: James, Billy, and Mary were gone by then. He was the only one living in Lonesome Bay at that time.

Annie and I were married and living in Pedro Bay when this terrible thing happened. Nicolai had come down to Pedro Bay to visit. It was fall and so he decided to go bear hunting. He took George Jacko, our nephew, with him to hunt bear up Iliamna River. George was about 15 years old. Well, they went up to Iliamna River and these Aleuts[5] from Newhalen were up there on the River also. These Aleuts didn't know Nicolai and George were up there. That is the year that Johnny, our son, was born. Annie was in Anchorage then to have him. So it was the late fall of 1947.

Those Aleuts, the guys that shot him, brought Nicolai and George back to Pedro Bay the next day. Sam Foss called Carl Williams on the radio and they got word to Anchorage and some FBI guys came to Pedro Bay. The Aleuts that shot Nicolai took those FBI guys up to the river and showed them how they made the mistake. They were sitting on a scaffold waiting for a bear. There were about three to four guys with rifles sitting up on that scaffold. Nicolai and George were drifting down the river hoping to see a bear. It was one of those darkest of nights. You know, that time just before the new moon. They were drifting slowly down the river and came near the Aleuts' scaffold. The boat scraped the bottom of the river sounding like a bear jumping into the water. The Aleuts didn't see that skiff. They just started shooting. George said they were kicking empty gas cans around in the boat, too, but they (the Aleuts) didn't even hear it. George got shot in the neck. The bullet traveled right through him and came out again. Boy, good thing it did or he would have died, too.

Nicolai was dead when they brought him to Sam's dock in Pedro Bay.

Yeah, but I think if they could have kept him warm he wouldn't have died. They couldn't get him in the pilothouse of the boat. They couldn't get him in there to keep him warm. They just put a big tarp over him.

They said he died when they were coming across the bay. That's a long ways. They were way up to the forks of the Iliamna River. That's where it happened way up there on Iliamna River.

They got an airplane the next day that picked up George to take him to Anchorage. It was a floatplane. I think it was Levery Ross that was flying on the lake during that time. This was in the late fall, when the nights are the darkest.

No one was charged. The F.B.I. called it an accident.

When those guys that shot Nicolai went back to their village they never told anybody about what happened. One of the guys was an Apokedak. Another was a Nicolai, not sure what his first name was, seems like it started with an M. A third was a Freddy Olympic. About five or six years after this happened I asked one of Apokedak's sons about what happened. And he said he never heard about it. I said, "That's funny. You Aleuts must not talk much."

Nicolai was only 37 years old.

On Music

My brothers, Nicolai and Grasim, played guitar but they weren't very good. I think it was because they never played very much. Grasim had a phonograph and quite a few records. That phonograph was real big – tall. We listened to that a lot. I liked to listen to those records of someone

Hollie Foss with son Tommy and daughter Lulu in Pedro Bay.
(Photo Courtesy Walter Johnson.)

Nicolai's violin hanging on Walter's living room wall in Homer.

Buck Delkettie.

(Photo courtesy Walter Johnson)

playing guitar and singing. It sounded pretty good. I decided I was going to learn how to play guitar. It didn't take me too long to learn because I played it all the time. Had nothing else to do, so I practiced a lot. They got me started but I learned mostly by myself. I was about 10 or 12 when I started to learn. That guitar was so big I could hardly get my arm over it. We used to play Russian songs – picking. I remember Michael A Rickteroff played guitar. They never played very long or very much, so none of them were very good. It was a Russian style of playing – Russian tune.

We didn't start playing Spanish tune until one summer when Buck went to Bristol Bay. He went to the Bay before me because he was older. He learned from some Dagos[6] down there in Bristol Bay. That fall when he came back, he had learned how to play this Spanish tune. You know some of those Dagos[6] were musicians – they were good. That was where he learned how to play the Spanish style. He was pretty excited and so he taught me how to play that way. After learning this Spanish way of playing we never went back to the Russian tuning.

I played all the time. I would even take the guitar in the boat – like when we went down to Tommy Point with my brother Grasim or Nicolai. I would try to play while the engine was going. I'd press my ear against the guitar to hear my tunes. I played all the time because I wanted to learn and I wanted to be good at it.

Walter with his niece, Lillian Jensen, playing his electric guitar.

Walter playing his acoustic guitar.

(Photo courtesy Walter Johnson.)

I played my brother Nicholai's guitar before I got my own. My brother Mike played the accordion. He used to be pretty good. I liked listening to him play that accordion.

Buck and I played guitar together a lot. It was good, because we learned from each other.

I used to play with Holly Foss, too. He played the fiddle, you know. I would learn his songs so I could play along with him. Buck would play with him, too. Holly played for all the dances. That was fun to play along with him at those dances.

Nicolai tried to play the fiddle, too. But he didn't play it enough to really learn. I have his fiddle now. Well, that fiddle was falling apart, too. You know, when Nicolai died I don't know what happened to his house and all his stuff. But, Frank Rickteroff was over at Lonesome Bay and he saw this fiddle case sticking up out of the snow. He went to pick it up and it was this fiddle – Nicolai's fiddle. So Frank took it home with him. He fixed it up. He got it to where you could play the fiddle with the bow. Then he gave it to me. That was real nice of him. So I have it hanging on the wall here in my living room.

Don Stump asked me to start playing for the Native New Life Fellowship meetings in Anchorage.[7] So I started to do that. It was fun. I talked Buck Delkettie into coming along with me. He said, "No, I don't want to do that. I haven't played my guitar in a long time. The strings on it are all broken." So I told him to buy some new strings and come along. Well, he did. I don't think he liked it much but he kept coming and soon became a part of the New Life Worship team.

I played at the Spring Conferences, too. That was a lot of fun. We had those conferences at Iliamna, then at Port Alsworth. Those were some good times. Whenever I was in Pedro Bay I would play at church for the music service.[8]

I learned to play the ukelele, too. Didn't play it very much, but it was fun to play. Yeah, I really like music.

On Mrs. Singka and Fedosia Carlsen

Mrs. Singka, Mary Jensen's great grandma died in a pretty good way. That winter in 1949 Annie and I were wintering at Loon Bay, we decided to go up to Pedro Bay in the late fall to visit Gus and Mary.

They were staying in Evon Rickteroff's house at that time. We slept on the floor. Well, during the night I heard Mrs. Singka coughing. Mary got up and asked her if she wanted water. Mrs. Singka said, "No, that won't help." She died that night, didn't seem like there was any suffering. I don't think anyone even knew that she was sick. She seemed fine.

Fedosia, my mom's cousin, married this guy from Seldovia and they went to live there. Well, he took her down to Port Moller where they lived for a couple years. Then he brought a boat all the way from False Pass to Iliamna Bay. That boat ended up on the beach in Cottonwood Bay. I don't know what happened to it but we would always stop by and look at it when we went over there to see Bill Duray.[9] We would go over there to buy things like clothes and stuff. He ran like a second hand store there.

Yeah, Fedosia moved back to the Old Iliamna Village after her husband died. She lived in a little one-room house. She had a pretty hard time living there in the Old Iliamna Village. She had three kids: Phina, Louise and William. William died when he was pretty young, I think, from food poisoning. After Phina married Frank Rickteroff, Fedosia went and lived with them over at Pile Bay, for a short while, but their house

Group of Pedro Bay kids in 1949. Victor Nicolai holding hands with May Carlsen, tall boy is Alvin Foss, in white skirt is Thelma Jacko, Bertha Jacko behind her, Trygve Olsen behind Bert Foss in knit cap, Pauline Kolyaha in scarf, Ethel with ribbon in long hair, Gladys Carlsen, Manuel Rickteroff, uncertain who the small boy is. Boy with his head turned is possibly Mike Jensen.

(Photo courtesy Mary Jensen)

Mrs. Singka and Fedosia Carlsen.

(Photo courtesy Walter Johnson)

there was pretty small. Then she went to live in Pedro Bay in Gillie Jacko's little house. Gillie had built it to be a steambath. She had a stroke so Phina's girls, Louise and Gladys lived with her to take care of her there in Pedro Bay. Then she moved up to Nondalton. That was where she died. Gladys and Louise married guys up there and stayed there in Nondalton.

Foxie Kovaliak

Foxie was Evon Kovaliak's brother. Evon Kovaliak was from Newhalen. Evon was known as Brown Eyed Evon.[10] Their mother was from Kokhanok, she married a man from Seldovia and went to live there. For some reason Foxie was raised in the orphanage in Seldovia and he learned the Indian language there. When he was in his 30s he moved to Old Iliamna Village. His mother came over to live in the Old Iliamna Village also. She lived with Fedosia's parents. Not sure what the connection here was but Fedosia had also married a man in Seldovia, a Carlson so they must have been friends.

Foxie worked on the Princess Pat Freighter – freighting from Homer to Iliamna Bay before he moved to the Old Iliamna Village. He came to Old Iliamna Village with just a packsack full of his stuff. He lived with Annie's Mom, Wasalisa for a while before moving into an empty house that was my brother Grasim's old house. My brother had built himself a bigger house.

Foxie was always dressed up so neat and smelled good. He wore perfume. Annie used to wash his clothes – the perfume was so strong that she couldn't wash off the perfume.

Foxie never married as far as I know. He was the last one to move out of Old Iliamna Village – to Pedro Bay. He worked in the cannery in Bristol Bay until late in the fall. Then he would sail back up to Pedro Bay. I remember he would bring a lot of stuff home with him in his boat. He gave most of it away. When he moved to Pedro Bay he moved into the house in Foxie's Bay. This is across from where Norman Aaberg now has his house. The house belonged at one time to Tom Owens. I think he was the guy that built that house. Then Trygve Olsen, Annie's first husband, lived in it for a few years.

Foxie was the last one to live in that house in Foxie's Bay. The house burned down on him. He made a lot of bivak (home brew) down in his cellar. He had a lantern down in the cellar to help keep his bivak warm. We think that was how the fire started. We saw the smoke from the village of Pedro Bay and ran down there. It was in the winter. The house was burned up by the time we got there. We saw his tracks in the snow go from the house to a tree to get some limbs to start the fire then the tracks went back to the house. We think he must have started his fire and fell back to sleep and the fire in the cellar caught the grass and burned the place down. He wasn't even gray – his hair was pure black. He must have been around 50. I think that fire was either 1949 or 1950.

The Village Calls For a Preacher

You know about those invisible people or spirits? The village of Pedro Bay called a preacher from Tyonek, Dick Mishikoff to talk about those. He was with the Russian Orthodox Church and he came and preached about that. He said it was in the Bible about where those spirits came from. In Genesis, something about when Cain killed Abel. These spirits were cast out – because of that bad thing Cain did. The wandering spirits were Cain's people. They had no place to go so they wander around.

Nick Mishikoff with one of Gus/Mary's children in Pedro Bay.
(Photo Courtesy of Mary Jensen)

Whenever someone gets near them they feel a scary creepy feeling – they just get very scared. You know, where the hair on the back of your neck goes up. I only had that happen to me one time. It was when I was up the Iliamna River, up past the falls.

Dick had a brother, Nick that came with him. Nick ended up staying with Alec & Zenia Kolyaha in Pedro Bay for a couple of years. Nick Mishikoff and another guy from Tyonek were in Pedro Bay at the time that Foxie died in that house fire. This fire happened sometime around 1949, I think.[11]

Living on the Kvichak

1952 was the year I built a house there on the bank of the Kvichak. Chester Horton, my sister Virginia's first husband, used to live there, too. My house was way up on the bank, pretty close to where Chester and Virginia lived. It was a long way to haul water. But I liked it. You could see all of the flats. You were able to see the ducks, geese, moose, - it was really nice to be able to watch all that activity on the river.

Well, Pat Pattersen bult this house right after he married Emma Roehl there in Naknek.[12] Pat sold it to Andy Woods, I bought it from Andy. I tore it down and hauled it up to the Kvichak Flats and rebuilt it there on the bank. This was right after fishing. We needed a place to live, because I had sold our house in Pedro Bay to Carl Jensen. So I guess I was in a hurry to get it built. I rebuilt that house in 19 days, sometimes I had to work by flashlight, but I got it done. It was a nice little place.

Our house was quite a ways below Igiugig. It was about a mile from the Wasencarie's house.[13] A guy was also living in the old house that my Dad, Mom and I lived in over on Kaskanak River. It was the house I had been born in. It was so old that the guy living in it cut the legs of the chairs off because the ceiling was too low. His name was Art. I don't remember his last name. Lots of guys used that old house through the years. One day I decided to go with Ole Wasencary to check his trap line down on the Kvichak. Sometimes in the winter you can't get to your trap line for a week, because of weather or other things. Well, he found a wolverine in the trap. That wolverine was frozen from his chest down, but he was still alive. I don't know how he stayed alive like that. This was way down the Kvichak.

Wasenkari family
in 1936.

(NPS. Lake Clark National
Park & Preserve. LACL H-1294.
Donated Ellen Pike, 1998)

Ole lived there on the Kvichak ever since he married Mary Seversen.[14] He already had a house built down there on Ole Creek before he married Mary. I don't know how long they were there, and then Mary left him. He drank too much. He used to make his own brew. He was a white man, but I don't know where he came from.

That spring on the Kvichak we were listening to the radio one evening – listening to the ice pool going out up in Nenana. Right there on the river there was a moose and a young one. They were trying to get up on the ice. They were swimming. That is the time I missed the ice pool by about 5 minutes. Earlier I had gotten some ice pool tickets and sent them up to Nels Hedlund.[15] I sent him the tickets and wrote down all the minutes that I wanted. I told him to take them to Iliamna. He and Gus were there at Iliamna when the ice was going out. Boy, they thought sure I was going to win. The ice started to move a little too quickly. It stopped - it got hung up and then it took off again. Missed it by five minutes. Anyway, that was just a memory of watching that moose and her calf trying to get up on the ice while listening to the Nenana Ice Classics on the radio.

We stayed in that house one winter.[16] Left the house and never did go back. I don't know if it is still standing or not.

Moving to Homer

I had always liked Homer and wanted to live there after seeing it in 1942. Aunt Valun and her husband Charlie Roehl had moved there from Iliamna back in the 1940s. So in 1955 we decided to move to Homer. We went over there and I bought the land and built a little cabin. We stayed in it for only a short while.

On Becoming A Born Again Christian

I guess I used to be Russian Orthodox until the missionaries came and started teaching us different. We used to go to the Russian Orthodox Church there in Pedro Bay. But those Russian Orthodox priests smoked too much and drank too much. There was no change in their life. Nothing. They used to have their cigarettes in their pockets and would leave the church and smoke outside and then they would go back into the church. I think they would get drunk on the communion wine while they were back there behind that curtain. You know, how they had a little special room in the front of the church. This room had a curtain for the door and only the priests could go into that room.

I became a born again Christian in 1955 right here in Homer at the Christian Community Church. Yeah, Annie was already a Christian.

I quit drinking that same year. I was 33 years old. I had been married for nine years. I never even thought about it, quitting drinking. You know, it didn't bother me like it did a lot of other guys. I don't know why I even drank because it made me sick and it used to make me so mad when my older brothers drank. I quit smoking at the same time and that didn't bother me either.

I was baptized in Pedro Bay, I think sometime in the early 1990s. The pastor at that time was Pastor Hayes.

Anchorage – 1955 to 1962

We had earlier applied for jobs at the Alaska Native Service Hospital in Anchorage, you know before we moved to Homer. Well, they hired us and so we moved to Anchorage later that fall of 1955.

We bought a house in Mountain View. It was one of those basement houses. I always got the summers off to go fishing. Annie stayed in Anchorage through the summers and worked. She was a seamstress at the hospital. I was a helper in the laundry room.

When I went to work at the hospital I didn't have a birth certificate. I had to get one. Aunt Valun helped me get that because she was present when I was born. You know when I went to work at the cannery they helped me get a social security card but my birthday was wrong on it. I had been celebrating my birthday on June 27. Aunt Valun told me I was born July 14, 1922. We got that changed.

Oh, not too long after we moved to Anchorage, Annie needed Ruthie's birth certificate. She couldn't find it. So we called Heinie Roehl, Aunt Valun's son. He was living in Homer at that time. We asked him to go over to our little cabin and look for that birth certificate. Well, he went over there and there was no house, just a burned up pile of stuff. I guess, someone had moved in there and ended up burning the place down.

Well, we lived in Anchorage for seven years, both of us working at the hospital. We had good jobs, we both liked working at the hospital.

The kids went to school there in Anchorage. Yeah, we lived there for about seven years then we got tired of it and decided to move back out to the Iliamna Lake country.

Spending A Winter In California

In 1962, we had a pretty good fishing season. Since we had the money we decided to do something different and went to live in the Los Angeles area for a year. We drove down the highway. It was just Annie, Ruthie and myself. We left Johnny and Howie with Ethel and her husband, John Adcox there at our house in Anchorge. When we got to California we stopped at a small town south of Los Angeles. We rented a house and Ruthie went to school there that year.

Walter with Ignatia Delkettie's sister and her family in California.

(Photo courtesy Walter Johnson.)

We enjoyed ourselves there. You know, we would take drives just to see the country. On one of these drives we found Ignasia Delkettie's sister.[17] She had married and moved to California. Yeah, we stopped to visit her and her daughter was there, too. That was nice.

In May we drove back up to Alaska, because I didn't want to miss the fishing season. That was a nice trip and a nice place to stay. Weather is pretty nice – never changes.

Moving Back to Pedro Bay

So in 1963 we moved back to Pedro Bay. I bought my brother Gus Jensen's place and we lived there for five years. Ruthie went to school there her eighth grade year. Mr. Cousineau was the teacher then. She went to high school at Victory Bible High School.[18]

Barney Furman was in Pedro Bay then and he helped us get her into that school.[19]

Yeah, Gus's house needed a lot of work when we moved into it. Our first year there I spent a lot of time just fixing the place up. Then the second year I added a living room

Gus Jensen's place in Pedro Bay. House that Walter bought.

(Photo courtesy of Walter Johnson.)

Gus/Mary Jensen, Carl/Marge Jensen, Walter/ Annie Johnson, Dolly Foss Jacko, Valun Rickteroff Roehl, and Gillie Jacko in Walter and Annie's house in Pedro Bay.

(Photo courtesy of Walter Johnson.)

on the front, you know the lakeshore side. David Victoroff and Charlie Roehl helped me build that. Aunt Valun and Charlie stayed there in Pedro Bay with us for about a month. They sure liked being there.

After I got the place fixed up I started to trap again, mostly right around Pedro Bay, like Knutsen Bay and Pedro Creek. I trapped mostly mink and marten.

I think it was the third year we were there I built that cabin up on the river – a trapping cabin. Annie and I would stay there for short periods of time while I trapped, mostly in the fall.

I put up a quonset hut down by the beach there in Pedro Bay, too. I got all the materials for free from Naknek. You know all the tin. The metal was curved. I built the frame out of two by four studs, then I put that tin right over it. Worked out fine. That was a good storage place.

I built a dock there, too. It is nice to have a place for people to dock. You know most folks traveled around in boats at that time. I also needed a place to dock the *Hornet*.

We liked to travel around the lake after fishing season was over. We would travel around on the *Hornet* – you know to get fish, pick berries, trap and camp. The *Hornet* was nice because it was a good place to sleep when we traveled around the lake.

Prospecting

You know when Ernie Zink first moved up to Pedro Bay he lived over in Knutsen Bay for a couple years. There was a cabin there that he lived in. He cooked for a cannery down at Bristol Bay.[20] I don't know why but he just started coming up to Pedro Bay.

Well, he had a trap line that ran up the Knutsen River. He said he thought there was some gold up Knutsen River. He said when he walked his trap line he went by this rock all the time and it looked different than the other rocks. So he knocked some pieces off of it and he found something that looked like gold. He sent these pieces out

Ernie Zink standing in front of his home in Pedro Bay.
(Photo courtesy of Walter Johnson.)

to Anchorage and got a letter back from them that said that it was gold. So, yeah there is gold up there along Knutsen River. He said this rock was right on Knutsen River in a place where another little creek ran into the river.

Another guy came through the country. He knew rocks, you know minerals and he said he thought there was gold in some of the mountains. I don't know who he was.

Yeah, there were others that would look for gold, too. Carl William's sons would go out looking.[21] One of his sons, I forget which one, had a little machine for finding gold. He made this machine while he was living in Pile Bay. He came down to Pedro Bay and showed me how it worked. He told me about how he checked most of the creeks all the way down to Tommy Creek, but he never found anything.

Yeah, so when we moved back to Pedro Bay in 1962 I would go out and look for gold. I would hike in the mountains around Pedro Bay. Boy, it is nice. You know it is so flat and easy walking once you are up there on the mountains. You can see so far. I really enjoyed walking around the hills and mountains. I never did find anything that looked like gold.

I walked around up above Pile River, too. But I never found anything. I also walked around the hills above Tommy Pt. Someone said there was gold over by Pope Vanoy. I think it was already claimed, but it was never worked.

I went out quite a bit but just never found anything. I did it for quite a while. We used to hear a lot about people looking for gold. So I guess I decided to have a look for myself. It was a good thing to do even if I didn't find anything.

Living in Tommy Pt.

In 1969, after Ruthie graduated from high school we moved to Tommy Point. I always did like Tommy Point. It was an easy place to get berries – the island out front was just loaded with blueberries and cranberries.

We liked to camp out a lot, too. We would travel on the *Hornet* around the lake to pick berries, and just camp out. We would go up to the Iliamna River, to William's Creek. This is across from where the Pedro Bay Corporation has a cabin. We would set the net to get our fish. Haul it back to Tommy Point. One time I had a pretty good load – over 500 fish. We ate some of it and smoked the rest.

One year Elia Anelon of Iliamna wanted some fish pretty bad for his dogs. He had a lot of sled dogs. I wanted to buy a 4K Diesel generator. He said he would sell it to me for 800 fish. We had lots of fish – we had a big smokehouse and no dogs. We smoked the fish – unsalted so it was good for dog food. That was what I used to trade with him for the generator. I gave him 800 fish and 100 bones.[22] The light plant (generator) was good for a long time. I think it is still there. Ruthie and Lanny used it when they lived there.[23]

I think we lived there at Tommy Point for about six years, just Annie and I. We didn't have a house when we first moved there. So we lived in a little cabin at Tommy Creek while I built a place at Tommy Point. First I built a smoke-house down at Tommy Point. Then I built us a tent to live in. We didn't have a regular tent but I had a lot of canvas that I used to build us a tent. I put windows in it, because the canvas was

Dome home almost completed.

(Photo courtesy Walter Johnson.)

so dark. We lived in this for most of that fall until we got the dome built.

That dome was good. I thought it would take a long time to warm up but it didn't take long to heat. It was 14 feet high.

Someone built it in Intricate Bay. He had bought the kit and put it up there at Intricate Bay. I got to know the guy when he was living there. Anyway, the BLM told him he had to move out of there because he didn't own the land. He took it down and stored it over at Kokhanok in Billy Rickteroff's warehouse. Yeah, I bought that dome, loaded it on the *Hornet*, and hauled it over to Tommy Point. I built it all by myself.

It didn't take me too long to put it together. I worked on it every day. I made a mistake on the first row. Because of that mistake I had to take the whole thing down and start over. Each piece was a triangle and was numbered. You had to be sure to put each piece in the right place. After that first mistake, everything went real smooth. I got it done that fall and so we lived in it that winter.

Annie and I lived in our Dome for about six years. That Dome didn't last long after we left, though. It started leaking.

On A Reef!

One day we decided to take a run up to Kokhanok Bay. It was a beautiful day, so we thought it would be a good time to visit Danny Roehl at his place. I was going pretty fast and the sun was in my eyes, so I couldn't see the water very well.

The *Hornet* on a reef.

Walter's Tommy Pt. "ranch" in late fall.

(Photo courtesy Walter Johnson)

Boy, I was going fast when I hit that reef! There we were out of water. Well, I called Gabe Olympic over there at Kokhanok. He came right away in his fishing boat, but he was pretty drunk. Good thing he had a guy named Andrew with him. Andrew didn't drink. They pulled me off those rocks and I headed straight home, back to Tommy Pt. When I checked the bottom of the boat there were no holes. That was something else.

Time To Leave

It is late fall so the water is pretty high. See how the dock is partly under water. I had to make a bridge out to it. Also the slough behind us is flooded. This was a high water year.

Yeah, we enjoyed our time there at Tommy Pt., but we decided in 1978 that it was time to move back to Homer. I was 56 years old.

Transformed

A Distant Memory

This is another story of those invisible people. Mrs. Sinkga told me this one. This man went out hunting. He built a scaffold. He was sitting there on his scaffold waiting for a bear and it got dark on him. Pretty soon he heard something walking. He couldn't see anything because it was so dark. So he just aimed at the noise and shot. After he shot whatever it was just hollered like it was a human. The first thing he thought of was _____. He must have shot a _____. He didn't know what to do so he went home and told his wife what happened.

He did look around before he left the place, He looked at the place where he had heard the noise but he didn't see anything. He checked to make sure there wasn't a person there.

Well, it wasn't long and he started to get these pains. They were so bad that he could hardly stand it. Everyday he was just getting worse and worse. The village people became scared of him. He was getting hairy. His fingernails were getting long. They didn't know what to do with him. He was in pain all the time. They partitioned off a room with split logs, lumber that they hewed off and put together. They fed him through a little window they made in the wall.

His fingernails were long and he started scratching the walls. They were afraid he would weaken the logs and get out. Then he started to pass out. He would fall down and pass out for a few minutes. The people that were living in this big building got together and wondered what to do with this man. They decided that the next time he passes out they were going to get him and take him out and burn him. They weren't going to kill him or anything.

You know a long time ago they used to burn people when they died. They didn't bury their dead; they burned them.

So they got a bunch of dry wood, limbs and stacked it up and fixed it so that they could just put a fire in there and get it going really quick before he woke up. So that was how they got rid of that man. He did try to get up because he woke up but it was too late. They had him tied down. He couldn't get out of the fire. He just burned up.

Next morning it snowed and they went over to see if he was burned up. It looked like a bunch of people had come during the night. The snow was all tramped down with people's tracks. They were the tracks of the _____. They had come and got him. They had taken him away.

Camping, Trapping, Hunting

Lonesome Bay Mountain

First camping trip I remember was when I started going up the mountain with my mom. I was around seven years old. Old Fedosia Carlson and sometimes Annie's mom, Wasalisa Mysee, would go with us. Fedosia was Phina Rickteroff's mom. She and my mom grew up in Old Iliamna Village. Fedosia and Mom were friends and they were cousins.[1] Annie's mom, Wasalisa, was a friend, too.[2] She didn't grow up in the Old Village, though.

Mom sewed really nice coats and things with the furs. We ate the meat, too. It was good, Mom cooked the ground squirrels without salt. She didn't care for salt; we didn't use it much.

We picked lots of berries: cranberries, blackberries, and blueberries. There were lots of those big berries, like raspberries, too.

My older brothers: Grasim, Mike, and Gust helped us out, after my Dad left. I learned trapping and hunting from my brothers. Yeah, they were often in Lonesome Bay with us. But, most of the camping that I did early on was with my mom up on Lonesome Bay Mountain.

Gust and Nicolai would help us get our camp set up on Lonesome Bay Mountain. They would come with us and help us set up then they would go back down the mountain.

This one spring my mom and I and old Fedosia were trapping squirrels up on the mountain there above Lonesome Bay. I was about eight, so I was old enough to run back to Lonesome Bay to get groceries. I'd run back down to the house to get some more supplies like tea and sugar. Mom had a pretty long trap line. So we stayed up there a long time and we would run out of groceries. One morning I got up real early and took off down the mountain to our house in Lonesome Bay. I ran all the way down the mountain to our house. When I got down to the house Nicolai was there, I don't know if Gust was. He might have been still sleeping. It was early in the morning. I got what Mom wanted me to get and put it in my pack sack, then went back up the Mountain. I got back to the camp, put the supplies into our little tent, then I went after Mom. I caught up to her before she got to the end of her traps. I used to like to run all the time. This was why Gillie never did like to take me along with him on hunts.

Becoming a Good Bear Hunter

One spring while we were camping up on the mountain my brothers and Gillie got a bear. Well, my brother Nicolai Jensen and Gillie Jacko killed this bear up on the side of the mountain, quite a ways from our camp. The same direction we would go to check our snares. There was a big swamp below our camp. Gillie and Nicolai had come with us to set up our camp and they saw some bears there on that swamp. They went down there to kill them. There was a sow and two cubs. They killed the sow. So this is what Gillie told me. He said, "If you want to be a good bear hunter and not be afraid of bear,

Gus Jensen, Pete Trefon, Buck Delkettie, and Walter Johnson up Pile River Valley.

(NPS. Lake Clark National Park & Preserve. LACL H-576. Donated by Walter & Annie Johnson, 1994)

you go and rub your head on that bear's forehead while he's alive." Well, just as soon as that bear dropped I was all ready to do that. But I made sure he was not going to get up.

I Was a Pretty Good Shot With the .22 Rifle

One day when I was around 14 years old, my aunt Sophie, my brother Grasim's wife, asked me to hunt some spruce hen for her. I said, "Okay." She gave me 15 shells for my .22 rifle.

My other brother Gust Jensen and his friend, Paul Zachar, were out hunting for spruce hen, too. Paul was often visiting us. He was Wanka Zachar's son, Zenia Kolyaha's brother. They lived in the Old Iliamna Village.

Well, I went over towards Lonesome Bay Creek and found some spruce hen. I shot 14, missed one. I brought my Aunt Sophie 14 spruce hens. Guess I was a pretty good shot.

Gust and Paul didn't get anything that day.

Beaver Trapping with Nicolai and Gillie At Kaskanak Creek

I was about 15 years old on this trip. It was the winter after we lost Mom. I went beaver trapping with Gillie Jacko and my brother Nicolai.

I ran all the way from Lonesome Bay to Kaskanak Creek. They only told me once that I was young so I had better run. After they told me that I didn't try to ride with them, I would just run. So I ran all the way.

We left Lonesome Bay early, made it to Iliamna in one day. We stayed overnight there. Next morning we took off, made it to Lower Talarik Creek. We stayed overnight there and left pretty early that next morning. They told me where to wait for them. They told me I'd come to a big sand bluff, and it was real long. Right down at the end of it there is a little cache sitting on the beach. They told me to wait there. We would stop there and cook tea before we went over the hill to go inland. So that was what I did.

Once I was going I didn't want to stop running. When I wanted to see how far they were behind me I would run a circle to see where they were, then I would just keep going. I didn't want to stop, didn't seem to get tired or thirsty.[3]

We didn't take any breaks during the day except that one stop before we went over the land into Kaskanak Creek. The days were long so the traveling was good. I guess we wanted to take advantage of that.

It was about six miles inland to Kaskanak Creek from those sand bluffs. We didn't even have a tent. We stayed under a tree. We found a tree that had lots of limbs that went way over. It was short but really nice to stay under. It was very dry. We added to it, you know, we put more limbs to make it more waterproof. Then we put some spruce boughs down to sleep on. That was our camp for a month.

Walter's older brother Nicolai Jensen and brother-in-law Gillie Jacko. They are traveling down the Lake to Bristol Bay and have stopped at one of the islands, probably to look for seagull eggs.

(Photo courtesy of Walter Johnson.)

Some Aleuts from Newhalen were trapping there along Kaskanak Creek, also. We would visit them sometimes at their camps.

After we were done getting our beaver skins, ten each, we walked back, brought all the dogs back with us. There wasn't any snow so we left the sled behind. The dogs were all loose, you know walking with us. When we got to Iliamna, we stayed at the Roadhouse. Hans Seversen always had a place for us to stay. I'm surprised our dogs didn't run off or get into a fight.

We fed them dried fish that we carried with us. When we were in the camp we fed them cooked beaver meat. They were strong. I think they could have pulled a dogsled, even on bare ground. Three or four of the dogs carried dog packs so they helped us carry our stuff.

I think this was around the first of April. The ice went out in May, so we walked along the beach all the way from Kaskanak Creek back to Iliamna, then on up to Lonesome Bay. Going back up to Iliamna took us three days. The days were even longer now. Walking along the beach was good walking, nice gravel beaches.

We stopped at Talarik Creek, about a mile inland from the beach. We stopped there to visit Steven Sours or Sava.[4] We had tea with him. Nick Olympic was visiting, too. He was also trapping in that area by himself. After we had coffee with Steven we headed on up to Iliamna. The days were so long, you know we just kept going. Got someone in Newhalen to take us across the river with a boat.

The next day we made it on up to Lonesome Bay. Most of the creeks were pretty low or even just dried out. So it was good walking. We made it in five days from Kaskanak Creek to Lonesome Bay with our furs and dogs.

Trapping and Hunting Alone

One day I decided to go up to Iliamna River by myself to trap. I went up in a little knock down skiff with a five-horse motor on it. I went up to the forks. I think I took my skiff down the river and then walked back up. Bears were gone then. This was in November. I stayed there for 17 days without seeing anybody. Really nice, you know. You are all alone. It is nice and quiet. You can do anything you want to do. I was just waking up one morning when I heard a .22 rifle shot. It was my brother Nicolai. He said he was out checking his traps so he walked over to my camp. He knew where I was because I had told him where I would be. I think he was just checking up on me. He had a trapping camp on Pile River. I think he spent the night there then walked over to check on me.

Others times I would pack my packsack and go off hiking somewhere by myself for several days. I would go up Pile River and hunt for bear. Never saw many bear. There weren't many bear around then. Way up Pile River, there is a trail that takes you to Tazimina. I built a scaffold up above the ground there. I wrapped my blanket around myself and lay down and listened for bear. I never heard anything. All of a sudden I sat up and here there was a bear coming down the trail. I hadn't even heard him. He went off into the willows and was gone.

Another time, I made a camp at Bear Creek and then I went further up river, (the last place to hunt bear), I went up there and I watched for bear. It got so dark I couldn't see anything so I was thinking I should go back to my camp. I was about 16 years old.

It was dark and I couldn't see. I made it back to my camp but it was really hard to see anything, see the bear, you know. It is dangerous, especially when the wind is blowing against you, he could smell you but you can't smell or hear him. One had to be pretty careful. That was a dangerous night when I had to make it back to my camp in the dark. Good thing there weren't any bear around that night.

Turned Our Leaky Tent Into A Canoe!

One spring, Gust, Buck and I decided to go beaver trapping down at Kaskanak Creek, that place where Nicolai and Gillie took me a couple years earlier. I was about 17, Gust was 22 and Buck was 18 when we went down there.

We walked to Iliamna from Lonesome Bay, packing all our stuff in backpacks. When we got to Iliamna, Harvey Drew was there, so we got a ride with him. He was driving a large dogsled that we all fit in. Harvey was the oldest of the Drew boys. He was trapping down in Lower Kaskanak with his whole family. His old man, Mrs. Drew, and the girls were all with him at the trapping camp. But I think he went back to Iliamna to get some supplies and that was how we got a ride from him.

He dropped us off by the mud bluffs. From there we walked inland to Kaskanak Creek. This must have been in late March or April. We set up our camp there along Kaskanak Creek. It is about 18 miles from Igiugig on the Kvichak River. Once during our stay there we had to walk over to Igiugig to get some groceries. Hermann Sandvik owned the store there at Igiugig at this time. We had no dogs, so he gave us an old dogsled to use. It was no longer any good for dog team use, but it had good runners. It sure helped us a lot. We put all our groceries into it and then pulled it all the way from Igiugig to our camp on Kaskanak Creek.

We stayed there at our camp on Kaskanak Creek until May, when the creek went out. That was when we decided to make a canoe with our tent. We made the frame from birch and small spruce trees. It was pretty big, had to be to hold all three of us, plus our beaver hides.

Our tent was like cheesecloth, whenever it rained the tent would leak. But when we put that beaver grease on it after we stretched it over our frame, it never leaked. We boiled the beaver fat down and made beaver oil. Then we burned dried grass, you know how it turns to charcoal when you burn it. We needed a lot of that. After we burned it then we would add it to the beaver oil while it was still cooking. We kept adding the burned grass and stirring and adding and stirring, until it turned into a thick paste. Then we took a rag and wiped it on the canvas that was stretched over our canoe. That made it waterproof.

Yeah, I don't know where I learned about that beaver oil and burned grass but someone told me about it and we decided to try it. Worked out pretty well. Sure was a lot nicer than packing all our stuff those 18 miles.

It was a lot easier to travel that way. We didn't have much freeboard but it worked out well. Took us all the way down to the Kvichak about 18 miles. Then we beached it, turned it over, and walked away from it. We couldn't go upstream with it, because the current on the Kvichak was too swift, you know. So we walked on up to Igiugig, it was only about 6 miles upstream.

There was a fur trader staying there at Igiugig. We sold him all our beaver hides. We each had our limit of 10 each. I think we each got a couple hundred for our hides. Then we got an airplane ride up to Iliamna with Jack Elliot. There were a lot of guys there at Igiugig waiting for a ride. There was Henry Roehl and his family, Buck, Gust and I. I think there were 11 of us in the airplane. It was a six-passenger plane. He was very overloaded. That Jack Elliot used to fly so low. You remember where Harvey Drew dropped us off, by those mud bluffs? Those bluffs must be about 30 feet high. Well, we were flying below that, we were just above the water. Boy, he flew low. Once he was flying so low he hit an owl.

Pile River Trapping Cabin

You know I had a cabin up there on Pile River, too. Effim Karshekoff, Joluk's grandson was with me. I think I was about 18. Effim was five years younger than me. He is Donkoo's son. We were up there to trap. I told Effim that we should build a cabin because it would be easier to stay warm.

Well, we had cut our logs earlier and when we went back up there our logs were frozen into the ice of the river. I hurt my back trying to get them out. I ended up staying in the tent two or three days because my back was so bad. Well, after my back healed and I could start lifting logs again we got them out of the river and up on the bank. Boy, those logs were so big it only took three logs to make it high enough for us to stand up in. With the roof on it was fine. It was sure better than a tent. It was warmer. I made a stove out of a gas can. Boy, when those gas cans get hot – they get red hot! Surprised they never fell apart.

This cabin was just below Bear Creek. It was back in the timber. We didn't use it after that one winter. I don't know if anyone else used it because it was hard to find.

We were trapping mink, fox, and martin, you know, whatever we could get. It got too cold, gets too hard to do stuff outside. So we gave up after about a month and went back to Lonesome Bay.

Effim didn't live with us. His parents were from Eagle Bay but he was often living with his Grandpa Joluk over there by the mouth of Pile River. No, Effim never lived with us. We didn't like to have him around because he stole too much. You know he was the one Sam told us to take to Anchorage and leave there. Sometimes Effim would live with his Grandpa Joluk when he lived there in Pedro Bay, too.

His dad, Donkoo was just as bad or worse. Donkoo lived down in Eagle Bay. Hugh Millet said he always had to watch Donkoo when he came to his place to visit.[5]

Tom Owens

I don't know where Tom Owens came from. He came to work on the road; when the Iliamna Bay road was being built. He was the cook for the road crew.

After the road project was done he stayed in the area. He would go down to Bristol Bay every summer and fish for the Dimond J cannery. In the winter he lived in Pedro Bay and trapped. He built a house there in the bay across from where Norman Aaberg has his house. It was the house that Foxie died in.

One winter I went trapping with Tom down at Peck's Creek. This is on the other side of Big Mountain. Alec Kolyaha, Gust Jensen and myself all went with him. Tom couldn't do much of anything. He just stayed in the camp. He had asthma pretty bad. But he had a cabin up there. I guess he must have built it himself. It wasn't very big so he stayed in the cabin and we stayed in a tent just down the hill below him. That hill was kind of steep. I don't know how many times he had to rest to get up that hill. He would be out of breath.

He came down to cook for us. He made us breakfast, good hotcakes. Yeah, he was a good cook.

We'd set the traps up on the line and check them everyday. We did well. We all got our limit. Beaver were good then. Tom showed us how to clean the beaver. Boy, that guy could flesh a beaver hide! You had to get all the fat off the hide, you know. When he finished one it was nice and clean – no fat. We all helped with the stretching because there would be four to five beavers a day. We made hoops out of birch and willow because they would bend without breaking. We used string. You tie the four sides to the hoop then slowly threaded the rest and stretched it until the skin was nice and round and taut.

Earling Anderson was there at Peck's Creek staying in Tom's cabin. There were also a couple guys at that time living down by Big Mt. They had a cabin on the shore there inside that big island. Sam Murray was one of them, don't remember the name of the other guy.[6] Well, they lived there a couple years I think – they also lived over at Iliamna for a time. They knew Tom and tried to get Anderson to leave, told him he had no business being there. But he wouldn't leave. So he was there when we got there that winter to trap. Tom didn't ask them to leave. Tom was a really nice guy. He said he didn't care. So the guy was still there when we left.

A Whistle In the Night

This happened when I was maybe 19 or 20 years old. I decided to go up to Iliamna River to trap, you know, for beaver. This was in the late fall. I took Carl Jensen, my brother Mike's son, along with me. He was just a little guy then but it was good to have him along. He could chop wood and keep the camp. I would mostly have him stay in the camp.

We set our tent up on the river bank there in the usual place where other campers pitched their tents. It is past the forks on the left fork, near the waterfall.

Well, we had been there several days already and I had some traps set out. I was down river from our camp when this happened. There is a big beaver dam quite a ways from the camp. I was out late because I was watching for beaver near this dam. It started to get dark so I decided I had better head back to camp. After I left the beaver dam I had to take a portage. This happened while I was on that portage. I heard this loud whistle. Boy! It sounded just like a human whistle! I thought of the _____.

That was when I got scared. Boy, I got so scared I got dizzy. I was even staggering like a drunk man. Then I kind of came out of it, you know that very scared feeling. I didn't want to be on the land so I went all the way back to camp by walking in the river, it was shallow so I could wade in it. When I got back to camp I didn't even tell Carl what happened. I didn't even make tea or nothing. I just crawled into my sleeping bag and went to sleep. And boy did I sleep!

When I woke up next morning I was fine. A couple days later I went back up there and there was nothing. It was fine. You know I think it was an owl I heard. It was just so sharp and getting on toward dark that it really scared me.

Later I was talking to Gory Nicolai about what happened and he said the same thing happened to him in that same place. Only he wasn't alone when it happened. I don't remember the name of the person he said was with him but they both got scared in that same place.

Froze to the Bottom!

Gust and I went beaver trapping the winter of 1947 down to Peck's Creek. This is on the other side of Big Mountain. We were both married at that time.

Yeah, we went all the way to Peck's Creek, the place we went trapping with Tom Owens. There used to be a lot of beaver there. Boy, it was cold that year, all the beaver lakes were froze to the bottom. You couldn't even set a trap for them. Every time we tried to cut a hole we would have to splice the handle of the pickax onto an extension just to reach down far enough to keep cutting the ice. Instead of finding water we would start hitting frozen bottom.

We spent nine days there. We couldn't find a single beaver house that was alive. I think they were all frozen. Trapping can be a tough job.

Mary Balluta Jensen (Gust's wife) as a child with her family—Mr. Singka (her great grandma's second husband), Mrs. Agafia Singka (her great grandma), and Marfa, her mother.

(Photo courtesy of Mary Jensen.)

Copper River

One winter I took the family over to Copper River. There was a log cabin there. I bought it from Gregory Anelon. He sold it to me for 500 dollars. We trapped in there for a while. Ethel and Trygve were with us. That was the time Dennie Moore and his wife lived there too. He had built a house there where old Alec Flymn used to live. You remember when we moved Alec Jr.'s house over to Pile Bay? Yeah, Dennie took that picture.

Dennie Moore had a wife and I think he had a couple very young kids. He also brought six horses with him. Boy, those are strong animals. He used those horses to

Walter's illustration of a martin set.

pull logs out of the woods to build their house. His wife would ride the horse while it pulled logs. But they lost all their horses. They didn't have a barn for them and ran out of feed. The horses just wandered away. The wolves must have got them. Only one survived.

Then Dennie went to Anchorage to work. This was the winter we were there so he asked me to take care of the horse. He would send a hundred pound bag of feed to Iliamna. So we took care of it until he came back that spring. He took the horse over to Newhalen, but it was mistreated and died. Then Dennie got a fishing job down Bristol Bay that summer. I am not sure what happened to him after that.

Yeah, it is pretty hard to make it there at Kokhanok Bay, especially when you don't have a boat. Dennie didn't have a boat. I am not sure why he came out there to live.

Cold and Miserable

About two years after I got married, Gust and I went up to Iliamna River to trap. Boy, it was cold! It was a good thing we didn't freeze, living up there in that wall tent. We used to hook up our dogs and go up river toward the waterfalls on the left hand fork. It was really cold bucking that wind. I bet it was 60 below up there in the mountains. We were trying to get some martin. We got a few – maybe six. They are easy to trap. You chop a tree down and leave a high stump. Then you pull the tree over the stump, this makes the head of it go up higher. Then we hang our bait on the end of the tree and set the trap right on the wood of the stump. Martins don't know what it is. They just step right into it. Then they would fall off you know when they struggled and the trap would fall. When you got there to check it they would be hanging there dead.

We stayed a little over a week. It was too cold and miserable. Not too many martins either.

Wading Through The Snow!

Another time we went to Peck's Creek, Gust and I. We went down with a dog team. It was really cold. The trapping wasn't very good. I don't think we got many beaver that year. It was something else to get home. This was the year Alec and Zenia Kolyaha were camping at Loon Bay. We stopped there for the night. The next morning when we woke up there must have been two feet of fresh snow on the ground! There was so much snow we had to walk ahead of our dogs. You know, you had to practically wade through the snow to make a trail for the dogs. We headed on up to Pedro Bay but stopped at Flat Island and unloaded all our stuff and left it there. We traveled all day and night, didn't get home until early the next morning. I think it took us about 16 and ½ hours from Loon Bay to Pedro Bay. We got home at around four or five in the morning. No snowshoes! That was some pretty tough traveling. That was the last time we went to Peck's Creek.

Trapping Cabin On Old Iliamna Village Site

In 1967 I built a little cabin on the Old Iliamna Village site. No one lived up there on the river at this time so there was a lot of game in the area.

The next year Annie and I went up there to trap. Our kids were all gone by this time so it was just the two of us. We were up there for about two months and we got

Walter's trapping cabin on the Old Iliamna Village site.

(Photo courtesy of Walter Johnson)

quite a few mink, otter, and beaver. I think this was October to December. It was the year that Wien plane crashed there in Pedro Bay.[7]

Yeah, the lake wasn't frozen up until late that year. I remember we had a lot of fog. The river froze up. It was a nice little time there on the river.

The only visitors we had were Arthur Roehl and his brother Willis.[8] They came up just after I had shot a moose. I had to go and check my trapline line so I told them to follow my tracks and go get themselves some moose meat. The moose was across the river over behind the Foss place by the mountain. They went and got what they wanted and took it back to Pedro Bay with them. I would go in and pack out what we needed, took quite a while to get it all. There weren't any wolves around. I had all the meat hung up on some trees and it froze so it was fine. Yeah, nothing bothered it.

After that Wien Air crash there in Pedro Bay there were a lot of airplanes flying around. One of those planes landed on the ice in the river right in front of our cabin. The pilot told us about the airplane crash. We were about ready to go back to Pedro Bay so I asked them for a ride. They gave us a free ride back to Pedro Bay.

Store Burned Down

A Distant Memory

"This happened while all the people of the Old Iliamna Village were over on the Inlet side in their camp there. They used to go over to the Inlet every spring to dig clams and get other seafood. There wasn't much to eat over in the Old Iliamna Village during the spring. They would stay at the camp there on the Inlet side until the salmon came into the Lake.

The people camped on the other side of the point on the right side of Iliamna Bay towards Cottonwood Bay. That mountain was so close and steep, there was a nice waterfall running right down the mountain where they had their camp. So they had fresh water right there.

It was a real nice place to camp. All gravel. There was a lot of beach. They walked over there when the tide was low. It was good walking at low tide.

Well, the store was burned down this one spring while everyone was over on the Inlet side at their camp. There was a man that couldn't walk living in the village. He was left there alone, while everyone else traveled over to the Inlet. I don't know how he used to get around. He used to roll around like. I don't know how he got out of that store after he set it afire. Anyway, he went back to the states, wherever, he came from. He was a white man. I don't know his name. They lost a lot of money from that store. They think he stole it all and burned the store down. Then, somehow, he left, went back to the states, I guess. That was what they said.

When the people came back to the village the store was all burned up. Boy, they lost a lot of stuff and money. This was while my mom was a teenager, so it would have been sometime in the 1890s."[1]

Sailboats being towed by tugboat in Bristol Bay. This would be what Walter saw on that stormy day.

(Photo courtesy Walter Johnson)

Commercial Fishing
In Bristol Bay

Started Young

1936, Age 14: This was my first time going to Bristol Bay – I was 14 years old. I worked at the Dimond J cannery in Koggiung. That cannery is located at the mouth of the Kvichak. I did everything; split fish, piled cans. I traveled down to the Bay with my brother, Grasim on his boat, *The Advance*. That was how we traveled to Bristol Bay every year. He used it to haul freight up from Naknek, winter supplies, stuff for his store.

My brother Nicolai had a boat, too, one that he bought down in Bristol Bay. It was lengthened and he had a pilot house put on it and added a 12 hp engine. You couldn't fish it because it was too long. Nicolai used it to travel on the Lake and down the Kvichak to Bristol Bay.

1937, Age 15: I set net with Paul Cusma.[2] We bickered and fought all summer! It was just the two of us, but boy, we couldn't get along! We didn't fight on the boat. We would go up on the dock to fight. Physically fight up on the dock because we would have a disagreement and so we would fight about it. Paul was a hard guy to get along with. We made it through the summer, though. We were the same age. We made our own money. The fish price that summer was 12.5 cents a fish. Started that season off at six cents a fish. But everything was furnished; grub, boat and nets. You rowed. You rowed and threw out your net. We had to row everywhere. We just picked a spot to fish and put our nets in. There were no fishing permits or set net sites at that time.

1938, Age 16: I fished with my brother Nicolai in a sailboat that year. This was good because I learned to sail. It was just Nicolai and I, so I learned a lot that summer.

Once it was blowing so hard we couldn't fish so we anchored up. There were a lot of

Fishing sailboats in Bristol Bay.
(Photo courtesy Walter Johnson)

boats out there. We anchored up for the night. The next day was a Saturday and we got that day off. So, we thought we better go up to the cannery. We had fished the whole week. We hoisted our sail and we were sailing up to Koggiung. We passed all these boats that were upside down because of that big wind –an east wind. I don't know what happened to the fishermen, there were seven or eight boats upside down in the water. We never heard anything about what happened to them. We didn't have anything like safety boats, but we did have lifejackets – they were good ones – made from cork. We made it into the cannery that day. We felt lucky after seeing all those boats.

Another time we had about 200 fish in the boat. They were good ballast – good for sailing. We anchored up. Our anchor wouldn't get a hold – the bottom was so hard it wouldn't let the anchor get a hold on the bottom. We had to splice a lot of line to our anchor line so it would get a hold. We were anchored up and watching these sailboats trying to get to the scow. We saw some getting blown about and drifting right into the scow. We called them bunk scows. They had a pilothouse and sleeping place. They were for the fisherman. You could eat there and sleep there. These two guys were drifting into the scow. They had a bridle on the chain. The boat hit that bridle and a big wave took the boat and lifted in right up onto the scow. The guys jumped off and the wave came again and lifted the boat back into the water – the guys were not on the boat and it blew out to sea. They never saw their boat again.

Another time a tugboat was towing seven sailboats in to the dock. It couldn't move because of the wind. We watched it disappear off the horizon. Don't know what happened to it. Pretty bad situations happened back then because we had no power – we were at the mercy of the wind and storms.

1939, Age 17: I fished with my brother Nicolai again. It was another good year for me because I was learning how to do things.

1940 & 1941, Age 18 & 19: Fished with my brother Gust both years.

Fishing My Own Boat

1942, Age 20: Got my own boat this year, you know a cannery boat. Simmie Zachar[3] fished with me, boy he was hard to get along with, too. Gust joined me for a short while that summer.

We would just row and throw out the net. We had to row because we still didn't have engines. I didn't own a fishing boat but used a company boat. I think Gust got a furlough from the army and that is why he came and fished with me for about a month. Yeah, we fished together. We were still using sailboats then. We got pretty strong by the time the fishing season was over, just from pulling net, rowing the boat, pulling in the loaded nets without a power roller, we had a roller but it wasn't powered. The roller just rolled by itself. We didn't have to hang the nets very often because the cannery usually had nets for us to use. At that time if you made 1500 dollars, that was a good season. It was a lot of money.

1943, Age 21: Fished for myself again, got my own boat from the cannery. This year Simmie fished with me, but he burned his hand real bad, So, I had a white guy for a partner, Joe Anders. He took Simmie's place. We fished for Libby's Cannery. For a partner Anders was good because he was a hard worker. He fished before, so he had experience. He never got his own boat. He would fish for people that got sick. Take their place. He made good money. I had him all summer on the boat.

We had a limit of 1600 fish per boat. I wasn't very experienced on loading

Gus Jensen & Walter fishing in Bristol Bay.

(Photo courtesy Mary Jensen)

a boat. We were down to Koggiung. It was always good fishing down there. So we decided to go down there. We were rowing because there was no wind. We had two nets, 75 fathoms each. We tied them together and put them out. They were 'smoking'. We left them for about 15 minutes, pretty soon there was no more net. It was sunk. We had to pull it in. We had to pull in on the roller by hand. We filled the stern. We couldn't put it all into one bin because it would tip the boat. We had to go from one bin to the other as we pulled in the net that was loaded with fish. We pulled it all in. We had left the net out too long. The boat was heaping from stern to bow with fish. We had 3700 fish! We anchored up and started picking the fish out of the net. It was pretty difficult. We had to put the fish on top the net. I told Joe, "Let's go to the scow." There was one pretty close to us. There was a light wind, so we sailed over to the scow. Once we made it to the scow we pewed out 1500 fish. Then we parked the boat behind the bow of the scow and picked the rest of the fish out of the net and then pewed that out onto the scow. There were 3700 fish total. We had way over the limit, since we were only allowed 1600 fish. So, we had to give the rest away. I think we gave it to Holly Foss. He was fishing that year. He and Frank DeSilva[4] were partners. Well, we didn't do that again.

It was a good thing we didn't swamp. We put gloves into our oarlock holes, this kept the water from coming into the boat. Swamping was always a problem, seemed to happen to the Dagos a lot.[5] I think because of lack of experience. Yeah, it could happen so easily, you know if the wind came up quickly.

1948, Age 22: James Rickteroff, Goolia, fished with me this year. [6] It was okay. He was a little clumsy on the boat because of his bad leg, but he was fine. His sister, Mary, was carrying him around when he was little. She slipped down on the ice and broke his hip. It never healed right.

1945, Age 23: My brother Gust and Joe Anders fished with me. I think it was because Gust was still in the army and just got some time off to fish for part of the season. We didn't have to go anyplace but stayed right in Coffee Creek. Fished for the Koggiung cannery. Good fishing there when the tide was low. We got 31,000 fish that season. They were paying 14 and ½ cents a fish that year. The canneries did not pay by the pound for fish until after the change over to powerboats.

1946, Age 24: This was the year Annie and I married. I fished with Benny Foss in a sailboat.[7] We had our guitars in the boat. When we'd get stuck on a sandbar we'd play guitar and sing all night or until the tide came up to drift us off. Once we fished all day and it was getting dark. We had about 1200 fish in the boat and we tried to get to the tender but couldn't because it was too calm and we had to row, just couldn't made it. So I told Benny we should drop the anchor and wait out the night, then deliver the next day. Woke up to daylight but it was very foggy, couldn't see anything. So we were just lying down, resting and waiting out the fog. Pretty soon I heard someone hollering, they thought we were sleeping. It was the Alaska Packers tugboat and we were right in front of him. They couldn't turn to miss us and it was coming right at us. I got out of the forecastle head as soon as I heard him hollering. I saw the tugboat with two scows on each side just plowing waters straight for us. They were going up to Koggiung. The tugboat captain shifted the engine to reverse to slow down. He slowed some but he was still coming pretty fast. I called Benny and told him we were getting run over. He came out. Just before it hit I jumped on the bow of the scow. The tugboat hit the boat right in the middle. Benny jumped and grabbed the rope fenders on the tugboat and clambered up the bow of the tugboat. Our boat was drug quite a ways before the tugboat was finally able to slow down. Cracked the deck of our boat but other than that it didn't hurt the boat so we were able to continue fishing it. We asked the tug to tow us up to Koggiung so we could deliver our fish. They did, it was about five to six miles. Only other thing broke was our rudder and that was easy to replace.

High Boat in 1949

I took Trygve, my stepson fishing one summer. We were fishing in an open skiff in Nakene, just below Koggiung. We were high boat one day. It was blowing East wind. Most fishermen were afraid to go close to the shore because they were afraid of washing up on the beach. We had an outboard motor, but we were drifting, you know while we were picking the fish, and we got close to the beach. Well, I didn't want to go dry (end up on the beach), so I just took a knife and cut the net. It was loaded with fish. Then we pushed the boat out and went out to the scow. There was a scow close by and we went to it and delivered our fish. It was a good place to fish, on the cut bank. Trygve was soaking wet from all the splashing. I was wet, too, but I told him to stay on the tugboat, so he could dry off. I got the monkey boat to take me back to the beach and I told them I would tie a rope around the net and he could pull me back out. I did and it worked out. The net was full of fish. I pulled the net in and we went back to the scow. I tied up on the leeward side of the scow and picked my fish then delivered it. We put in 2000 fish that day, just by making drifts along that beach. We would go back and forth. Make a drift by that cut bank and then delivered to the scow.

Trygve Olsen and Mike Jensen in Pedro Bay.

(Photo courtesy of Walter Johnson.)

I didn't know but I was high boat that day. That next morning when I went to the post office the bookkeeper saw me and told me to come into the office. "Hey!" He said, "You better slow down a little bit. Yesterday you got more fish that all the fishermen with the big boats fishing out there." I think Trygve was around 12 years old that year. Yeah, I ended up high boat that day.[8]

We drifted in the open skiff that summer, fished in Koggiung a lot. I fished in the open skiff because

Bristol Bay fishing boats.

(Walter Johnson)

these would be the only boats the cannery had for us to use, an open skiff with an outboard motor. We would come in every night to rest and sleep in the cannery. This was after I sold my converted sailboat.

I used company boats throughout this time. I never took my kids, Johnny and Howie, fishing. Actually we did take them once. Gus took Johnny, my oldest son, and I took Howie, my younger son. But they were pretty young and weren't much help. I didn't do that again until they were grown up. We both did all the work ourselves. They were more worry than help.

Switch To Powerboats

1950: This was the year they started allowing powerboats – fishing boats with an inboard engine. A lot of fishermen didn't know how to handle the powerboats. Made it difficult for them. It was okay fishing in powerboats, I had been in powerboats before so I was sort of used to them. Several of my brothers had powerboats. I still fished in a sailboat the first year they put engines in. I fished by myself. I did that a lot, especially when the fishing season was poor. That way I didn't have to pay a partner.

1951: I never fished in a company boat that they put power in – that the cannery put an engine in. I bought a sailboat and put my own engine in it. So in '51 I

Walter on a "monkeyboat." He found this in dry dock in Homer.

(Photo courtesy Walter Johnson)

fished a sailboat again, but that was the year I bought a sailboat and an engine. Yeah, they had all these boats just sitting there at Nakene. No one wanted them because they were too big to row and handle. So I decided to get one and put an engine in it myself. The engine was a 25 horsepower engine. I had the cannery hoist it into my sailboat after the fishing season. Then I got towed up the Kvichak River to Iliamna Lake.

That was the summer Annie stayed with Rose Hedlund in Chekok while I was fishing.[9] After I got back up to Iliamna Lake from Bristol Bay I pulled that sailboat up on the beach there in Chekok by Nels and Rose's smokehouse. That was where I put the engine in. Boy, that was a lot of work. I had never done anything like that before. Tried to get Nels to help me but he said he never did that kind of work before either and he didn't want to ruin it. So I didn't get any help from him. Nels was a carpenter, said he didn't know machines.

Yeah, well you know, when you make up your mind to do something, you can do it.

So, I did it. Kept me pretty busy. You have got to get the shaft in straight, make sure the engine is straight for the shaft. It was pretty tough to do. A lot of it I just figured out as I went. It worked when I was done, so I guess I did it right.

I used that boat for fishing the next two or three years. Then I sold it. I got 800 bucks for it. I think that was 1954. That was the year we decided to go over to Homer. I had always liked Homer ever since the time I stopped there in 1942 on our trip to Anchorage aboard the Princess Pat.

1955: I sold my converted sailboat because I wanted to move to Homer and I didn't have any place to keep the boat. I sold it to someone in Naknek. It was easier than storing it.

The *Hornet* on its test run in Seattle.

(Walter Johnson)

1960: I bought a skiff from Sonny Groat of Naknek. I could get 700 fish in it. That was a good load. Fished that boat for a couple years.

The *Hornet*

1962, Age 40: This is the year I bought the *Hornet*. After I bought the *Hornet* I fished alone quite a few years. Annie helped me some, but I did that because there weren't many fish. I think I did that the first three years that I had the *Hornet*.

For a couple years I left the *Hornet* at Nelbro Cannery. They would have mechanics there that would make sure the engines were good. For two years I did that then I started taking the boat up to Iliamna Lake. It was better to take the boat up the lake. I liked the trip up the lake and it was nice to have the boat on the lake to run around in through the fall. You know, take little trips around the lake. That was nice.

Taking a Chance Pays Off

One time we were pulling in a good load over by that gravel spit. This gravel spit is over across from the mouth of the Naknek River. Boy, it was blowing a hard west wind.

Johnny Kankaton[10] fished with me that year. We put out our net and we got a good load. Only had about four inches of free board. We had to watch that pretty close but we made it to Naknek without swamping. We picked our fish and put it all in the scow. There was another boat from our company there and he was picking his fish, too. You know some of these guys don't know how to pick fish. Well, this guy was cutting his fish out with a scissors. We finished up and then we went back over to that same place and got another good load.

We brought that over to the scow and that guy was still there picking his fish. He had a pretty good load and he was by himself.

Johnny Kankaton asleep after a hard day's fishing.
(Photo courtesy Walter Johnson.)

They had a limit on the number of fish you could get because the cannery couldn't can them fast enough. We usually got our limit. We would just fish until we got our limit.

Yeah, Johnny and I took a chance with the wind that day, but we got our limit so it was a good day.

All In a Day's Work

Another time the season was closed and they said they were going to open it when they got enough fish up the river. So we were in the cannery and I had my son Johnny fishing with me that year. He is a fast fish picker. They told us that they were going to have breakfast about 6:00 A.M. before the opening. We heard there were a lot of fish on the west side. So right after breakfast we headed out. We went right over to the west side and put out our net. And boy, the fish started hitting! They gave us a 3000 fish limit that day. The first net we threw out got us about 1500. We delivered that. Then went back and got another bunch. We picked that really fast and threw our net in again and got another bunch. So we picked our fish while we were drifting. Then we started back to the cannery and ended up meeting our scow on the way.

The deck hand on the scow tied us up alongside. We pewed[11] our fish up onto the scow. At that time, there were no brailers, so we had to pew all the fish into the scow. We turned loose and took off for the head

Walter's son Johnny Johnson and great grand nephew, Josh Jacko.

(Photo courtesy of Walter Johnson)

Josh mending gill net. Josh said he practically made several nets with all the net mending he did that summer. He was 14 years old.

(Photo courtesy Walter Johnson.)

of the river – for Naknek. We got back just in time for dinner.

We fished for six hours and we caught our limit of 3000 fish. Yeah, Johnny, my son, fished with me that season. He was a young adult then. This was after he came out of the army, before he got married. We worked hard and we got our limit that day.

The *Hornet* docked at Walter's summer home in Pedro Bay.

(Photo courtesy Walter Johnson)

Final Years and Retiring

1992, age 70: I think Johnny Kankaton and Josh Jacko[12] fished with me this year. My son Johnny was with us for a while, too.

1995: David Victoroff and Fred Roehl[13] fished with me this year. I think this was my last year. The years kind of get mixed up, you know. Anyway, I finally quit. I was done.

Fishing was a good job, you know. You were like your own boss. You could quit whenever you wanted, that was good. You would just go to the office, get your pay, and then take off for home. I usually fished as long as I could – as long as there were fish to catch.

You know I never missed fishing after I quit. It wasn't that my last year was hard – I didn't notice any difference. Nothing happened that made me decide it was too difficult. It was just time for me to quit. I was done. Commercial fishing had been a good way for me to make a living.

The Giant

A Distant Memory

"The Giant was looking for his sister. He took this big rock and he lifted it up. The foundation of that rock was square, you know, really squared off where the rock was sitting.

His tracks were big. They were sunk way deep in the ground.

His footsteps were as big as that of two of a normal man's footsteps.

He was nine feet tall. They found him. When they found him he was in a cave. He was dead.

People put stuff in that Giant's Rock on the road to Iliamna Bay. The Giant's Rock was destroyed, blown up with dynamite by the road construction crew.

Final Years In Homer

Moving Back to Homer

In 1978 we moved back here to Homer. I came over by myself from Pedro Bay with Alec Flymn to check out the place. Alec was running the barge then between Homer and Iliamna Bay. When I got to Homer I bought some lumber for a 14'x16' house. There were no roads in this area then. I hired a guy that had a knockwell.[1] It is a truck that can go anyplace. It had tracks. They hauled all the lumber in here. I told them where to put it and had it stacked up.

Alec said he knew a good house builder and where I could find him. So I found this guy, Theodore. I asked him if he could build this house for me. I also needed to know how long he thought it would take him. He said he could build the place in about a week. He would hire someone to help him. So I told him I would be back in a week. I went back to Pedro Bay. We waited for about a week over there. Then we came back over, Annie and I. We stopped at Alec's, stayed there, you know. We had come over with him on his barge. He told us he thought our house was done.

I went to check it out and sure enough the house was up. The doors and windows were in. But it wasn't insulated. So I worked on it and got it insulated. Then I put up plyboard and got the walls finished. Yeah, we stayed at Alec's until I got our house ready for us to move into.

After we got moved in I built another 14'x16' room on the end of it – had that done before Christmas. Now we had a bedroom. The next fall after fishing I built this whole part here – kitchen and dining room. It was the whole length of the first two buildings. I did most of the work myself. We hooked up to the city water and sewer.

Walter's home in Homer.

Walter & Annie in their home in Homer, Christmas '99.

(Photo courtesy Walter Johnson.)

Walter & Annie's summer home in Pedro Bay.

(Photo courtesy of Walter Johnson)

Everything turned out good. The other bedroom, I think it is 20 feet long. It is only about 12 feet wide. That didn't take too long to build. Lanny, Ruthie's husband, helped me build the frame. Then I boarded it up myself. A friend of Lanny's came over and helped me put the roofing paper up on the roof. I hired a plumber to do all the plumbing. I did most of the wiring myself but I hired an electrician to wire into the box. So it took about three years to build this. We paid for it as we built it. That is a good way to do it. But, yeah it turned out nice.

We brought our oil cookstove range over from Pedro Bay on Alec's barge. Don Shugak came by just in time to help me haul it to the house. We had to carry it all the way from about two blocks down, where the road ended back then. It was pretty heavy. We had to carry it a long ways. I was sure glad for Don's help with that stove.

Building a Summer Home in Pedro Bay

We didn't have a house there in Pedro Bay after we moved back to Homer in '78. So we didn't spend the summers there for about 5 years. We would stay in the *Hornet* as long as we could into the fall. It wasn't too bad. We liked camping.

I took Ethel's little summerhouse from Tommy Point and hauled it up on the *Hornet* to Pedro Bay and put it on the point. This was the first part of our house there.

Annie inside summer home in Pedro Bay.

(Photo courtesy of Walter Johnson)

Walter & Annie's granddaughter, Deannie, in Pedro Bay. See in background Walter's collection and use of driftwood to decorate his yard.

(Photo courtesy of Walter Johnson)

When we lived in Gus's old house we had a new addition put onto the front of it. It was towards the lake.

One day I told Carl I wanted to take that addition and haul it down to the point, so that was what we did. We put a big rope around it and he used the blade of the cat and towed it down there. I had foundation posts already put in where I wanted him to put the house. He hauled it all the way down and put it on the foundation. It came out just right. Then he came back around and pushed it right up against the other building. Everything came out just real straight. All we had to do was nail it – fasten it together. Then we started staying there for the summers. It made a nice summer place.

We liked being there in the summers. It was nice to be right next to the water. You know, in Homer we can't see the water from our place. Annie enjoyed sitting at the kitchen table there in Pedro Bay and looking out over the water.

Hawaii

Yeah, we made the arrangements before going over to Hawaii. You know we had to figure out where we were going to live while we were there. We also went to the pool here in Homer to learn how to float and swim in the water. That helped a lot. But Annie never swam. It did help her to be a little more comfortable in the water, you know, just to wade.

We went straight to Kona on the Big Island of Hawaii. We had rented a condo there and we stayed there for a month. Ruthie, Lanny, Trygve and Nancy were over on Oahu. Ruthie came over to Kona to visit us.

We didn't have a car because there weren't any available – I was too late to get one.

Babe and Mary Alsworth[2] were living there on the Big Island of Hawaii then and they came and got us for a visit. We stayed a couple days at their place. A funny thing happened when they came to get us. They had this cow on a long rope, you know, a tether. They also had all these beehives. Well the cow somehow got tangled in one of those beehives and knocked it over. Those bees got pretty mad – they nearly killed that cow with their stings.

Another thing happened while we were there. The volcano blew up. We climbed up on Babe's rooftop to watch it. We could see

Walter in Hawaii.

(Photo courtesy of Walter Johnson)

Walter in Homer pool getting ready for Hawaii.

(Courtesy of Walter Johnson.)

Mary Alsworth in her kitchen in Hawaii. She used a big wood cookstove range to do her cooking on.

(Photo courtesy of Walter Johnson)

Parasailing in Hawaii.
(Photo courtesy of Walter Johnson)

and just feel the heat coming out of there. Sometimes you could hear the rumbling down there.

There was this man that was from Homer over there at Kona. He had a para-sailing business. He built a wooden airport like structure out on the water. This was how they used to parasail – they needed something to take off of and land on. Well, I decided to try this parasailing. Ruthie wanted to go with me. It was fun. We went up for about 15 minutes. It was a windy day and I got down okay but because Ruthie was so light they had a hard time getting her down. Now I guess they just wind you up and wind you back in – lot easier.

There was a restaurant we liked to go to for dinner. They always had a dancer there for entertainment. It was fun to watch. One night they didn't have any dancers so they asked the cook to dance. Boy, he did a good job. He could really dance. He told us a story with his dance.

Annie with Hawaiian dancers.
(Photo courtesy of Walter Johnson)

Well, the man that ran the parasail business was killed not long after Ruthie and I went up. He got a rope caught in his engine prop. So he went down there to get it out, but for some reason he hadn't turned off his engine and after he got the rope off the prop, it started up and cut him all up - really bad. They cremated him and scattered his ashes out in the bay there in front of Kona. Boy, there were lots of boats out there for his funeral! He had a lot of friends there.

After Kona we went to Oahu and got a condo over where Ruthie and Lanny were staying. We stayed there for another month. This time I had a car so we drove all over that island. One day when we were driving around – Ruthie was with us, we came upon this little town with an airport. There were all these gliders there. I decided I wanted to ride in one. Ruthie went with me. Annie didn't want to do that. She stayed in the car and waited for us. Well, we went on that ride. Our pilot was a lady. Boy that was something! After the airplane let us go we just sailed all over. We would go down to pick up speed then back up to go over the mountains. We even sailed over Waikiki. So quiet – just that swishing, you know of the air going by. I really liked that. Then we went back to the airport and landed nice and gentle, after we landed the plane fell on its side.

Annie Johnson

(Photo courtesy of Walter Johnson)

Annie Gets Sick

Yeah, one summer while I was fishing and Annie was home alone there in Pedro Bay, she said something happened to her while she was in the smokehouse. She wasn't sure what was wrong but she didn't think she could get back to the house. When she told me about that experience after I returned from Bristol Bay I realized that I couldn't leave her alone anymore.

Annie with her daughters Ethel and Ruthie.

She got steadily worse. For a couple years it wasn't too bad. We kept going to Pedro Bay for the summers. In Homer the Center would help out. They would take her during the day. Then she had a stroke and wasn't able to talk or walk. After her stroke the Center[2] couldn't take her anymore because they couldn't provide that kind of care. We started having some ladies[3] come in to the house to help out. Ruthie and I did most of Annie's care. Ethel would come and spend a couple weeks at a time to help out, too. You know to give Ruthie and I a break.

That is a very hard kind of sickness that Annie had. It was very hard after she couldn't talk anymore.

Appendix No. 1

The Family of
Stepan Rykterov and
Marina Mikhailovna

Stepan Rykterov, referred to as Tomsk burgher of Kodiak, born 1778 in Russia and died August 3, 1847, at age 71, in Kodiak, AK. In researching the term "Tomsk Burgher" I found that Tomsk most likely referred to the city that Rykterov was from. It is a city on the Tom River in the Southwest of Siberian Federal District of Russia. It is one of the oldest towns in the area, established in 1604. The term "burgher" refers to the status of an individual. Generally meaning that the person is of some high standing in a community, not necessarily aristocratic or noble but in economic or legal standing, probably a leader of some sort.

Marina Mikhailovna (1787-1856) is listed as Aleut of Unalaska. I was unable to find out much about Marina, but because Unalaska was already being used as a Russian trading post by the 1760s it is very likely she is of Russian/Aleut descent. Mikhailovna is a Russian name.

Only three of their nine children lived to adulthood.

Savva #1 (Savelii), born 1813, died November 24, 1887, age 74.

Savva #2, born 1819, died at Mulchatna in 1882, age 63.

Ivan, born 1822, died 1888, age 67.

According to the confessional records Savva #1's brothers Savva #2 and Ivan lived in the Old Ilamna Village with him.

Savva #2 married three times. All three wives died. All but one of his children died while very young. A surviving son, Iakov of his second wife, Ekaterina Chaiuk, born 1852 left for school in Sitka in 1864. It is unknown what happened to him.

Ivan (Iakov, Ioann or Evon) married a lady from Ekuk, Anna Chikhigak. They were married at the Iliamna odinochka on July 15, 1851. Of their 9 children only three daughters lived long enough to marry: Anisiia, Mariia, Matrona. Anisiia married Creole Stefan Kandakov at age 22. When someone was referred to as 'Creole' that generally meant they were of mixed blood - Russian and Aleut/Eskimo/Indian. Mariia married Kodiak Aleut Mikhail Shaiaman at age 20, he died, and she died a widow at age 29. Matrona married a Dena'ina of Iliamna Matfei Nutnutnika in 1878 at age 18. It is said Anna Chikhigak drowned in a river (Iliamna River?) at the age of 40. No record of Ivan remarrying. He died of pneumonia 15 years later at the age of 67.

The children of Savva #1
Stepan Rikterov
(b. 1813 – d. November 24, 1884)

Lawful wife Glikeriia Mylykhchtaitna was born 1813 in Kultuk (Kani Island?). She married Savva #1 Rikterov on August 23, 1842. She died on 1888 or 1875. The Children: I put in bold those that lived to adulthood.

Glikeriia's Age	Child and Birthyear	Death of child
Age 20	Nikolai – 1833	Died June 27, 1843 at age 10
Age 24	**Mikhail – 1837**	Died 1903/04, age 67
Age 26	**Dariia – 1839**	Married 1877, Death 1939?
Age 28	Ignatii – 1841	Died of a cold May 25, 1899, age 55.
Age 34	**Ioann** – May 13, 1847	died (pneumonia) April 29, 1901 at age 45.
Age 37	Nikolai – February 3, 1850	Died 1876, age 21 or 25
Age 38	**Vasilii** – March 9, 1851	Died spring of 1928, age 77
Age 44	Irina – 1857	Died 1872 of a cold, age 15
Age 46	**Efim** – 1859	Died 1911-1919?, age 50s?
Age 55	**Aleksei** – 1868 or 1871	Died of paralysis in 1900 at age 32 or 29.

Mikhail

Mikhail married three times. His only surviving children were with his third wife, Mariia L'kuduktdit, b. 1867, a Kenaika of Kijik. She married Mikhail in 1900. Their two children were Tikhon, born 1903 and Agrippina, born 1901. After Mikhail died she married Nikolai Grigor'ev in 1907.

Dariia

Dariia married Petr Tuknil'tishin 1877 at age of 38. They had a daughter that died in infancy. Petr died around the same time. Dariia never remarried but lived to a 100 years. There is a well-known photo of her wearing a squirrel parka.

Ignatii

Ignatii married Anna Chugil'tin (1854 –1888). One son, Pavel, lived to age 25. He had a daughter, Evdokiia. Not sure what happened to her.

Ioann

Ioann (also known as Ivan or Evon) married a Dena'ina, Vasilissa Feofilova Dhiial'chsha b. 1849. They had two children that lived to adulthood. Feodosiia b. 1878, she married Nikolai Carlsen of Seldovia. The second daughter was Katherine b. 1892, she married a Dena'ina Ioann Tugnukidel'n in 1910. He must have died as she married Wanka Zachar and had Xenia and Paul Zachar. This is how Fedosia and Katherine were first cousins to Walter's Mom, Anna.

Vasilii

Vasilii is Walter's grandfather. See Appendix No. 3 for more on Vasilii (William).

Kos'ma

Born on December 27, 1856, died May 6, 1919, age 63. Kos'ma is listed as the illegitimate son of Ekaterina Khuinagal'nova a Dena'ina woman from Kustatan village. Arndt states, "In the Nushagak parish confessional lists, she (Ekaterina) begins to be identified as living in the house of Savva Rykterov #1 in 1856." Arndt also adds that Ekaterina has two teenage boys identified as Matfei and Petr, both listed as orphans. In the 1861-1868 records she and the boys are listed below Savva's household but not as his household. The records in 1876 list Ekaterina with the Iliamna Kenaitsy as a widow and Kos'ma is listed with the Iliamna Creoles as Kos'ma Rikterov. In the 1900 census his birthplace is listed as Cook Inlet, his mother's as Kuskoquim, and his father's as Kodiak. The listing of his mother as from the Kuskoquim does not appear correct as his mother, Ekaterina is listed previously as from Kustatan, a Dena'ina village on the Cook Inlet. It could be the recorder misunderstood 'Kustatan' for 'Kuskoquim'. The oral history said he was one of Savva's adopted sons.

Kos'ma married Ekaterina Annuin (1862-1888) an Alutiq. They had one child: Anna, born May 11, 1887.

Kos'ma then married his 2nd wife Mariia Malakhu, a Kenaika (1872-1909) on September 1890. They had seven children, none show up in later records.

Kos'ma then marries a third wife Dariia Uiutkha, a Kenaika (1891-?) She is listed as 19 when she marries Kos'ma on February 2, 1910. They are listed in the 1910 census,

None of Kos'ma's previous children are listed with him. Arndt feels that this would probably indicate that they all either died or were adopted.

Irina and Efim

It is uncertain if Irina and Efim are Glikeriia's as she is getting on in age, also it is six years since her last child, Vasilii (William) was born.

No death date found for Efim, but he married Agafia Byktaiutna, a Kenaika on 16 September 1890. They had six children, only three lived to adulthood.

Ioann (Evon) – b. June 15, 1892 –died 1948?

Marfa (Mary Jensen's Grandma)-b. January 30, 1894/5

Varvara (Vera Roehl) b. January 3, 1907

Effim shows up in the 1900 census with birthplace listed as Iliamna, father's – Kodiak and mother's Kuskoquim (Kustatan?). In the 1910 census his birthplace is listed as Iliamna, his father's as Iliamna and his mother's as Iliamna. The oral history said that he was also one of Savva's adopted sons. After he died Agafia married a Mr. Singka.

Hannah Breece mentions Effim in her book. She said he was the wise man of the village and blind. There is a photo of him in her book.

Aleksei

Arndt could find no birth record for Aleksei. She said he is listed as a child of Savva #1 Rikhterov beginning in 1877 at the age of 9. The 1900 Census for Iliamna Lake lists his mother's birthplace as the Kuskoquim and his birthplace as Iliamna, with his father's birthplace as Kodiak. This would indicate that Savva was either his biological or adopted father. Arndt indicates it seems unlikely that Ekaterina, Cusma's mother was Aleksei's mother.

It is also interesting that there is such a large gap between Aleksei's birth and the rest of the family. He was 9 to 12 years younger than Effim, and 12 to 15 years younger than William. Again the oral history states that Aleksei was Savva's adopted son. (Also the mother's birthplace of Kuskoquim could be a mistake as well, and instead be Kustatan. There are a number of times the birthplace is listed differently from one census record to the next.) Aleksei married Vasilissa (b. 1875) of Mulchatna in 1893. See Appendix No. 5 for more on their children.

Final note on Cos'ma, Effim, and Aleksei.

The records are not clear as to the parentage of these three.

Cos'ma for sure is Ekaterina's child not Glikeria's as the birth record states this. Because she shows up as being of the household of Savva #1 in 1856, it is possible that Savva is his biological father, but he is not listed as such on the birth record.

As for Effim, the record lists him as the son of Savva #1 and and his lawful wife Glikerriia, although because of the age of Glikerria (46) and the large span of time from her last child it seems unlikely that she is his mother. Effim also lists his mother as being from the Kuskoquim(Kustatan?) in the 1900 Iliamna Census and Iliamna in the 1910 census, Glikerriia is from Kani Island.

The records are even less clear for Aleksei. No record of his mother is found other than what shows in the 1900 Census where she is listed as being from Kuskoquim (Kustatan?). No birth record shows that Savva #1 is his father, but he is listed as a child of Savva #1 in 1877 when he is 9 years old. There is also a large gap in years between the birth of Effim and Aleksei, this makes it less likely they had the same mother. So, unfortunately, nothing definitive can be determined concerning the parentage of these three: Cos'ma, Effim, and Aleksei.

The records often show different information for birthyears, birthplaces, etc. It takes a lot of cross-referencing to determine what is correct or most likely correct. For example, the birthplace of Cos'ma's mother is listed as the Kuskokwim instead of Kustatan. It is possible the same mistake was made with the mothers of Effim and Aleksei.

My thanks to Katherine L. Arndt of the University of AK Fairbanks for all the time she put into combing through the confessional records to glean a lot of this information. I also used census records and what I had learned through oral history.

William Rickteroff with
his family in the Old
Iliamna Village sometime
in the early 1900s. The
small child could be
Valun, and she was born
in 1901.

(NPS Lake Clark National Park &
Preserve. LACL H-716. Donated by
Gus & Mary Jensen, 1995).

William (Vasilii) Savvin Rykterov

Born, March 9, 1851. Died, spring of 1928. William was the 7th and probably the youngest of Savva #1 and Glikeria's children. He married Mariia Semenova Bytskunyshin, a Dena'ina of Kijik, b. 1858- d. 1914/15?

I am not sure if that is correct that she is from Kijik. Parascovia Valun Rickteroff Roehl, their youngest daughter tells in *Our Stories Our Lives* of how her dad was traveling up in the Mulchatna area with his dad, Sava #1 and that was where he met Maria. They married on March 10, 1881 at Old Iliamna Village. Their children were:

Anna, born 1880. (Walter's Mom) Died fall of 1937, age 57.

Merkurii, born 1882, died 1884 at age 3.

Mikhail (William Mike), born November 4, 1884. Died 1933/34 at age 50?

Nikolai, born April 30, 1886. Died March 26, 1908 at age 22.

Mariia, born 1889. Died early 1930s, age 40s? (Buck Delkettie's Mom)

Stefan, born August 19, 1892. Died sometime in the 1920s, age 28/29?

Evgeniia, born December 27, 1894. Died April 1, 1895 at age 1.

Paraskeva, born August 5, 1901. Died June 1, 1996, age 95. (Valun Roehl)

From Fr. Vladimir Modestov journals, entry for February 9, 1897:

"In this settlement lives Creole Vasilii (William) Rikhtorov, who is trader in the store of the Alaska Commercial Company and who teaches the children reading and writing and especially prayers and the adults church singing."

From *A Schoolteacher in Old Alaska; The Story of Hannah Breece*:

Hannah taught in the Old Iliamna Village School from 1909 to 1911. Here are some of her comments concerning William.

"The most important building in the village, and indeed in all the country round about, was the home of Old William Rickteroff, the reader of the church. . . I came to think of William's home as the Metropolis. It was in the central part of the village and stood out conspicuously because of its size and neat, well-kept appearance. It was the center of all social life. Every Sunday night dances were held there. It was the assembly room for any other public gatherings."p. 94

"Old William was merely middle-aged, with a long, iron-gray beard." p. 95

"William and his wife looked to be nearly pure Russian." p. 95

Paraskovia Valun Roehl says in *Our Stories Our Lives* that she was the youngest of 12. Arndt was only able to find eight, and only six lived to adulthood.

Anna Rickteroff

Anna Rickteroff was born in 1880 in the Old Iliamna Village to Vasilii (William) Savvin Rykhterov (b.1851) and Mariia Semenova Bytskunyshin (b. 1858). Anna was the eldest. Here is a list of Anna's children.

Gerrasim

Anna had an illegitimate son, Gerrasim (Grasim or Chris) Sours born February 17, 1898. He married Sophie Roehl, daughter of Frederick and Marie Roehl of Old Iliamna Village. They had no children. He died around 1934.

Anna and Andrei L'Kutuch'kil

Anna married Andrei L'Kutuch'kil on February 11, 1900 at age 19. Andrei was a Dena'ina of Old Iliamna Village. According to the 1900 Census he was born at Lake Clark (probably Kijik). No children listed for them. No further mention of him, assume he died. Interesting note - he has the same last name as Mikhail Rykhterov's (1837-1903) third wife, Mariia L"Kutuck"kil. Census shows she was born in Kijik.

Anna and Charlie Jensen

Anna married Charlie Jensen, (b. June 1879, a Dane) around 1905. Had four children with him. Charlie is said to have left his home in Copenhagen at the age of 8 as a cabin boy on a ship. They had four children.

Mike Jensen – (1906-1945?).

Nicolai Jensen – (1909-1947)

Alma Jensen – (1912-1990)

Virginia Jensen – (1915 -__?_)

Charlie Jensen then left Anna and moved to the Kvichak. See Endnote No. 14 under the section: *Walter, On His Own* for more on Charlie Jensen.

Anna and John Pedersen

Anna married John Pedersen, a Dane. Had one child, **Gus Jensen**, born April 16, 1917. John got sick and traveled outside for medical help, but he died and was not able to return before that. It was not known where he went. Gus married Mary Balluta.

Anna and Alfred (Alf) Leondi Johnson

Anna married Alfred (Alf) Leondi Johnson (man from Estonia) and had her last child, **Walter Johnson,** born 1922. Alf was with them for 5 to 6 years. The 1930 census shows Anna is alone with the children, so Alf was gone by then. He built himself a house on the Branch River and lived alone there for the rest of his life.

Anna became sick with T.B. and died in the fall of 1937 at the age of 57. She lived her last years with her youngest son, Walter in Lonesome Bay, in the house that Alf built for them.

Aleksei Riktorov

Aleksei Riktorov, b. April 1871, married Vasilissa (Evon) b. 1875 of Mulchatna in 1893. I could find no other records of Vasilissa, other than the 1900 Census stating her father was from Mulchatna and her mother from Lake Clark. I was told her maiden name was Evon. No written record could be found to confirm this. These are her children.

Agrippina

Agrippina, born January 20, 1893, died June 17, 1899 of fever, age 9.

Anna

Ward: Anna, b. 1890, is listed in household of Aleksei and Vasalissa beginning in 1894. Arndt was unable to determine if this was the same Anna (b. May 11, 1887) listed as the child of Cusma Rikhterov and his wife Ekaterina Annuin, Aglegmiut. Arndt seemed to think that Cusma would have reclaimed her once he remarried in 1890 if she were still alive. Arndt also felt that the ward Anna was not the child of Aleksei as she was too old to be his. She believes there was an error in copying and her real birth year was 1884. This ward Anna later married Alexander Flymn February 2, 1904 at age 19, this supports her birthdate as 1884. Arndt was also unable to confirm that Anna was the child taken from Katmai at the age of 7, when (according to oral history) Aleksei traveled there and brought her back to Iliamna to live with him and his wife.

Michael A Rickteroff with his wife Jean and children – Florence, Annie, Tootsie, David (their ward, Tootsie's son), Linda. Child in Michael's lap unknown.

(Photo courtesy Walter Johnson)

Alec Flymn, Sr.

(NPS. Lake Clark National
Park & Preserve. LACL H-456.
Donated by Violet Wilson.)

Anna (Rickteroff)
Flymn.

(NPS. Lake Clark National
Park & Preserve. LACL H-466.
Donated by Violet Wilson.)

Wasalisa and her children, Annie, Lagaria,
Michael A, Sophie.

(NPS. Lake Clark National Park & Preserve. LACL H-694.
Donated by Bert & Edna Foss, 1995.)

She (Arndt) was unable to find any Anna of this age listed in the Confessional lists of Katmai. If 1884 is her birthdate, she would have been 10 when she began living with Aleksei and Vasalissa.

Michael C

Michael C (August 17, 1895 – 1930). Married Katherine Simeon. Had two children, David and Jenny.

Michael A

Michael A born September 15, 1899. Married Jean Karshekoff of Nondalton. They had 5 children; Florence, Tootsie, Victor, Annie, Linda, and a ward - David. (David was Tootsie's son.) Michael A died at Eklutna and is buried there.

Sophia

Sophia (July 30, 1901 – December 23, 1965). Sophia married Nick Kolyaha. She had one child, Alex Kolyaha with Nick. She then married Sam Foss and had five children

Annie Mysee and her nephew, Alec Kolyaha, 1920/21?

(Photo courtesy Walter Johnson.)

with Sam: Johnny, Dolly, Hazel, Benny, Marjorie, and Edna. Johnny died at age 18. They adopted Johnny Evon, child of Virginia Jensen and George Seversen.

Dariia

Dariia, born March 12, 1903. Not much is remembered of her. She appears on the school attendance records from 1909 to 1918, then I don't see her anymore. It may be she died in 1918.

Aleksei

Aleksei died February 14, 1909 of paralysis. Different records say he was either 29 or 32, but according to the birthyear cited in the 1900 census he would have been 38.

Vasilissa

Vasilissa was then remarried to a Dick Mysee of Old Iliamna Village.

Born to her was Lagaria on March 13, 1911 in Old Iliamna Village. Lagaria married Hollie Foss in 1938. They had three children; Alvin, Bert, and Tommy. Lulu was their adopted daughter.

Born to her was Annie on December 29, 1916 in Old Iliamna Village. This was Walter's wife. Annie's father was Sophus Hendrickson, Sam Foss's cousin.

Vasalissa died in Pedro Bay in the fall of 1950.

Appendix No. 6

Locations on Iliamna Lake

1. Lonesome Bay
2. Kaskanek
3. Iliamna Fish Village
4. Squirrel Village
5. Loon Bay
6. Eagle Bay
7. Goolu Lakes
8. Bear Creek
9. Goose Bay
10. Chekok
11. Knutesen Bay
12. Tommy Creek
13. Tommy Point

14. Peck's Creek
15. Big Mountain
16. Kokhanok Bay
17. Cottonwood Bay
18. Old Iliamna Village
19. Jack Durand's

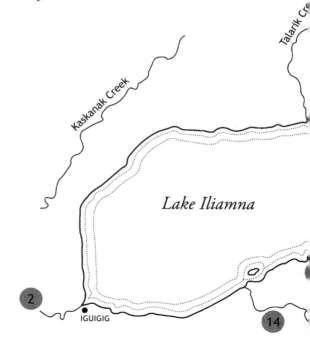

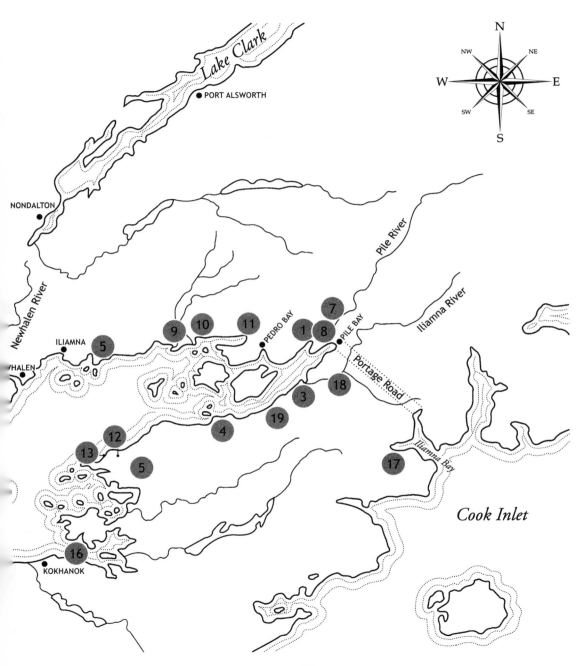

Appendix No. 7

Old Iliamna Village School Photos

1916

1916 Old Iliamna Village School Photo

I have been unable to find anyone able to identify the students. The lady in the apron is Mrs. Nash, the teacher. The person standing off to the side is Holly Foss. The students enrolled in the school that year were: Michael A Rickteroff, Steven Rickteroff, Sophia R. Kolyaha, Parascovia Rickteroff, Sophia Roehl, Daria Rickteroff, Marfa Evanoff, Ignatious Delkettie, Ephim Evanoff, Mike Jensen. Nickolai Rickteroff, Goverilla Rickteroff, Catherine Delcato, Wara Wara Rickteroff, Henry Roehl, Reaubell Zachar, Steven Sours.

(Photo courtesy Lake Clark National Park Service, donated by Marie Millet.)

1928

1928 school photo

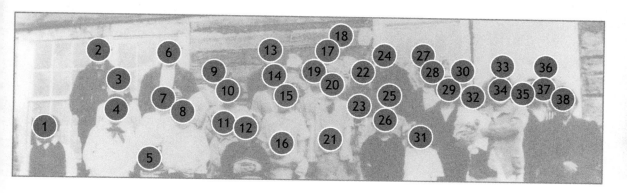

Old Iliamna School Photo 1928

1. Johnny Nezone
2. Old Hank Hinckley
3. Gory Nicolai
4. Johnny Foss
5. Mabel Zachar
6. Sam Foss
7. Paul Zachar
8. Drafim (Buck) Delkettie
9. Nikita Simeon
10. Lolla Rickteroff
11. Xenia Zachar
12. Hilda Simeon
13. Hugh Millett
14. Aggie Simeon
15. Annie Mysee
16. David Victoroff
17. Mrs. Johnston
18. Stephen Rickteroff
19. Lagaria Mysee
20. Phina Carlsen
21. Gladys Carlsen
22. Marie Millett
23. Lillian Rickteroff
24. Christina Foss
25. Frank Johnston
26. Frank Rickteroff
27. Stepenita (Evon's Wife)
28. Matrona
29. Mary (Rickteroff) Delkettie
30. Gadya Zachar (Wanka's 1st wife)
31. Dolly Foss
32. baby
33. Wasalisa Mysee
34. Annie (John) Rickteroff
35. Jenny Rickteroff
36. Mrs. Simmie Nikita
37. Katherine Rickteroff
38. Fedosia Carlsen

1930

1930 school photo

(Photo courtesy of Walter Johnson.)

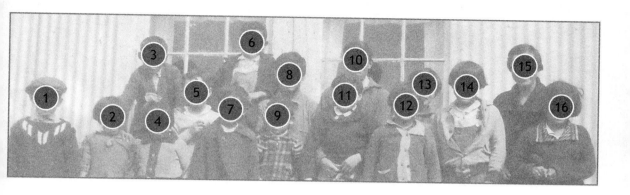

Labels for 1930

1. Tom Kinney
2. Xenia Zachar
3. Paul Zachar
4. Vera Rickteroff
5. Frank Johnston
6. Gory Nicolai
7. Frank Ricteroff
8. ?
9. Drafim Delkettie
10. George Seversen
11. Gus Jensen
12. Hilda Simeon
13. ?
14. Annie Mysee
15. Mary Seversen
16. Lillian Rickteroff

1930

1930 projects:

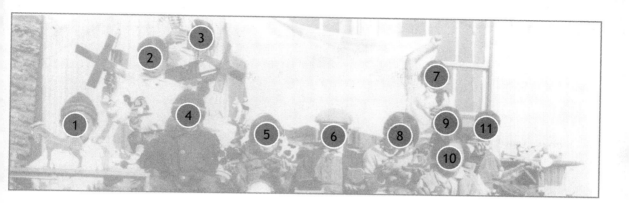

1930 School Projects

1. Drafim Delkettie
2. Paul Zachar
3. Bertha Roehl
4. Frank Rickteroff
5. Xenia Zachar
6. Billie Rickteroff
7. Annie Mysee
8. Hilda Simeon
9. Emma Roehl
10. Frank Johnston
11. Lillian Rickteroff

Endnotes

1. Townsend, Joan Broom, 1933, Ethnohistory and Culture Change of The Iliamna Tanaina. University of California, Los Angeles, 1965 Anthropology.

2. Branson, John. *The Bristol Bay Times*, "Iliamna Portage Long used by Bears, Humans," by John Branson, December 10, 1993.

3. Bancroft, Hubert Howe, *History of Alaska 1730 – 1885*, vol. 33, San Francisco, A.L. Bancroft and Company.

4. *Russian Exploration in Southwest Alaska: The Travel Journals of Petr Korsakovskiy (1818) and Ivan Ys. Vasilev (1829)*

5. Rikterovs were living in Old Iliamna Village by early 1800s.

    The marriage record of Savva stating that he married Lukeriia who was from Kultuk, a Dena'ina community would seem to indicate that he was already in the Iliamna area. This would mean he was there by 1842.

    The birth record of Iaonn, states that he is the son of baidarshchik of Iliamna odinochko Savva Riktorov and his lawful wife Lukeriia, born May 13, 1847. (Notes from Katherine Arndt.)

The Russian Orthodox priest/missionary, Hegumen Nikolai (1806-1867) traveled to Old Iliamna Village in 1847 to hear confession and give communion to Savva Rikterov, his wife Lukeriia, their children and thirty-two Dena'ina. Nikolai noted that there were forty-six residents in the village at that time. *Through Orthodox Eyes* by Andrea A Znamenski.

6. The Russian priest Modestov noted in his journal entry of February 9, 1895 that the settlement of Old Iliamna Village was "originally founded by Creole Savva Rykhterov, who was agent here under the Russian(American) Company and through it they transshipped provisions and goods from Kenai to Nushagak." Alaskan Russian Church Archives in collections of Archives, Elmer E. Rasmuson Library, University of Alaska Fairbanks. (Notes from Katherine Arndt.)

7. See Appendix No. 3 on William Rickteroff, Anna's Dad.

8. From the journal of Fr. Vladimir Modestov (Alaskan Russian church archives in Elmer E. Rasmuson Library, UAF) (Arndt's notes.)

9. *A Schoolteacher in Old Alaska* by Jane Jacobs, Vintage Books, 1997.

10. Unrau, Harlan D. *Lake Clark National Park and Preserve, Alaska: Historic Resource Study. 1994.* United States Department of the Interior, National Park Service, Anchorage, Alaska.

11. Alf Johnson was born in Estonia and raised in New York. For Anna Rickteroff, see Appendix No. 4.

12. *The Legacy of Pile Bay* by Donna Lane Associates. Bureau of Indian Affairs, Alaska Region Regional Archeology. January 2008.

13. John Coray (1926-1959) then went to Nondalton where he taught for two years.

From there he went to Port Graham for several years, finally gave up teaching and homesteaded on Lake Clark. In 1959 his plane disappeared over the Cook Inlet, never to be found. There is a book and CD out based on the recordings John Coray did of the songs of the Nondalton Dena'ina while teaching in Nondalton in 1954. The book is *Dnaghelt'ana Qut'ana K'eli Ahdelyax (They Sing the Songs of Many Peoples)* Published by the Kijik Corporation with assistance from the Lake Clark National Park and Preserve.

14. Walter is unsure of the exact year that he quit fishing. He thought his last year could have been when Fred Roehl and David Victoroff fished with him in 1994. However, another source says they remember him fishing in '95 with Fred and David. If that is so then he spent 60 years fishing in Bristol Bay.

Origin Of Old Iliamna Village

1. Oral tradition places this fort somewhere in the area of the village of Pedro Bay.

2. Branson, John. *The Bristol Bay Times*, "Iliamna Portage Long Used by Bears, Humans," December 10, 1993.

Walter's Early Life

1. See Appendix No. 4 on Anna Rickterov.

2. Oliver Millet (1865-1951) with his wife Theresa (1866-1966) show up in the 1930 Iliamna Census. He lists himself as a miner for gold and copper. He was born in Nova Scotia and she was born in Oregon. He was 65 and she was 63 in 1930. These may be the same people Hannah Breece refers to in her memoirs as

the prospectors for the Seattle mining company. Oliver and Theresa lived for some time above what is now called Millet's Pt. or Goose Bay.

Hugh Millet (January 29, 1892 – April 1, 1979), at age 37, son of Oliver and Theresa shows up also with his wife Maria, daughter of Frederick and Marie Roehl (July 28, 1901 – December 12, 2005) on the 1930 Iliamna Census. Hugh and Maria have three children listed; Gertrude (5), Jessie(3), and Julie (1). Jessie was later to marry Drafim (Buck) Delkettie, Walter's cousin.

Left Alone

1. On Goose Bay: Valun (Rickteroff) Roehl speaks about moving to Goose Bay in *Our Stories Our Lives*. She said they moved there in 1926 and lived there until their youngest daughter, Sophie, was 8 years old. Then they moved to the new village of Iliamna so Sophie could go to school. This must have been around 1940. From Iliamna they moved to Homer.

2. Walter's uncle, William Mike (Mikhail) Rickteroff was born November 4, 1884. Walter says William Mike moved from Goose Bay to Lonesome Bay in 1932. William Mike shows up in the 1920 Census at age 28, still single and living with his father William Rickteroff. He then shows up in the 1930 census, married with two children. So he didn't live in Goose Bay very long and he didn't live in Lonesome Bay very long either before he died, as Walter thought he was between 10 and 12 when his uncle died.

3. Annie John. A John family shows up on the 1930 Census in Newhalen. Evon and Annie John with their children: Anatastasia, age 20, Matlunda, age 13, Alexis, age 15, Wassili, age 9, and Ogaline age 8. The children; Alexis – age 17, Martha (Matlunda?) age 15, and Wasilia and Olive- both ages 10 show up on the 1932 Old Iliamna village School Attendance record. Annie John, age 26, is already

married to William Mike Rickteroff and they have two children as listed also on the 1930 Census. Annie is in the Iliamna Village School photo of 1927.

4. Frederick J. Roehl, Sr. (1860-1924), German born, moved his family from Koggiung to Old Iliamna in 1912. There was much talk of a railroad being built from Iliamna Bay to the interior of Alaska and it is said that this was the reason Frederick moved to the Old Iliamna Village. He died there in 1924 at the age of 64. He owned and operated the store there until his death. He was also owner of the Roadhouse down the lake that was bought by Hans Seversen. (*Seversen's Roadhouse: Crossroads of Bristol Bay, Alaska.* Edited by John Branson.) (U.S. 1920 Old Iliamna Census.)

5. William B. Regan shows up on the 1920 census of Old Iliamna Village. His birth year is 1870 and birthplace Wisconsin. Parents were born in Ireland. He had a brother with him, John M Regan. William's occupation was listed as Miner. Regan took over the Commissioner of the Iliamna District after Sam Foss got sick and had to step down. Regan was also Commissioner for the Naknek District when he moved down there.

    Dariia (Dareya or Dolly) Flymn, (b. 1907) was the eldest daughter of Alex and Anna Flymn.

6. Hugh Millet's last known residence was Anchorage.

7. See Appendix No. 3 for more on Old William Rickterov.

8. On Potlatches: There was a tradition of "Dancing Away the possessions of the Deceased." The possessions went to distant relatives. Valun speaks of this in her story in *Our Stories Our Lives.* She speaks of losing her mother's things with regret as does Walter when his mother's things were taken at the same type of event.

9. On Fedosia Carlsen: Fedosia (b. May 29, 1878 – d. 1950?) was the daughter of Ioann Savvin Riktorov (1847-1901) and Vasilissa Feofilova Chiial'chsha, a Dena'ina. Ioann was William Riktorov's older brother, this is how Fedosia was a cousin to Walter's Mom, Anna. See Appendix No. 2.

   Fedosia had a daughter, Mariia, born November 7, 1893 that died 1897. She had a son Dimitrii, born February 1, 1895 in Kokhanok. Not sure what happened to him.

   Fedosia married a Nikolai Baiu Carlsen of Seldovia on September 5, 1896. She had three children with him – Gabriel, died young but the two daughters, Louise and Phina grew up in Seldovia and were adults when they came to Old Iliamna Village.

   Louise was with Gory Nicolai for a while. Gory, after a day of much partying, went over to Iliamna Bay, a 12 mile hike. He stayed there overnight. Louise wanted him to come back and so decided to go after him. It was winter, people tried to stop her but she was very drunk and couldn't be stopped. The next day they found her on the trail froze to death. She had a dog with her.

   Phina already had her son Billie Barber with her when she came to the Old Iliamna Village and she was carrying Gladys. She then had Louise, May, and Lulu. Holly and Lagaria Foss adopted Lulu. Phina then married Frank Rickteroff and had several more kids with him; Herbie, Lorene, and Eleanor. She then left Frank and moved to Dillingham.

   Phina does show up on the Old Iliamna Village school records from the ages of 6 to 12. Then she doesn't show up any more. Louise doesn't show up at all here. It may be that Phina came back to the village initially with her Mom, Fedosia, then returned to Seldovia and came back to the village when she was an adult. (This information from interview with Dolly Foss Jacko 5-2-2010) (Pedro Bay Geneology Project done in 1986)(Old Iliamna Village School records)

10. Ed McDermitt shows up on the Lake Iliamna 1930 census. He is listed as a miner, age 47, born in Ohio.

11. Stephen Rickteroff shows up in the 1920 census, listed as age 28, but is not on the 1930 census, so must have died by 1930. Stephen's father, William, died in 1928 and Walter doesn't remember Stephen during that time. In *A Schoolteacher in Old Alaska* Hannah Breece speaks of Stephen *"the other son, Stephen, was crippled and much petted."* Page 95. Stephen is in the Old Iliamna Village School Photo dated 1928.

12. Another spelling used is Zacarooska as used in the 1912 Old Iliamna School Attendance records, where a Martha age 9 and Ephem age 5 are listed. Ephem must be the boy that drowned in Pip's Creek. Martha married Donkoo Karshekoff of Eagle Bay and had a son, Epheme. This is the Epheme that had much trouble as Walter recounts later.

13. Walter mentions at different times that he thinks someone is of mixed blood. It is interesting to note that Hannah Breece mentions in her memoir that "…all were of mixed blood, although, it seemed obvious, mixed in greater and lesser degrees."(pg. 99) If the slaughter of the men of the village story was true as told to Hannah this would be understandable. Also Old Iliamna Village seems to have been a crossroads, with many people passing through. See also note No. 1, *Walter, On His Own.*

14. Nastashia was the sister of Mariia Malakhu, a Dena'ina born in Old Iliamna 1872. Mariia was the second wife of Cusma Rickterof. The records state that both Mariia's parents were born in the Old Iliamna Village. Nastashia is buried in the Pedro Bay cemetery.

15. Wanka Zachar and his brother Homoshka were said to have come from Kenai in the early 1900s. They show up on the 1910 Old Iliamna Village Census at the ages

of 19 and 25. There was a younger brother that was to come behind them but he died. It is said they moved to the Old Iliamna Village because they had relatives there. Wanka, the oldest was born January 1885. Homoshka was born August 1891. Neither appear on the 1920 census. Then Wanka appears on the 1930 census. Wanka married Katherine Rickeroff (b. July 1895). She is the daughter of Ioann (Evon) Rickteroff (1847-1901) and Vasilissa Chial'chisha (b. 1849). Katherine is the sister of Fedosia Carlsen. Wanka and Katherine had two children, Xenia and Paul. Xenia married Alec Kolyaha. Katherine died so Wanka married Aggie Simeon and had another child, Mabel. Wanka then drowned while fishing in Bristol Bay.

Homoshka was married a number of times. He had two sons, Simmie and Feodor. Feodor apparently drowned while young. Simmie married and settled in Kokhanok.

16. Sam Foss (1881-1950) was the son of Baard (1850-1930) and Christina (1850-1940) Foss of Norway. Baard and Christina arrived in the U.S. around 1880. They lived in North Dakota for a time, Sam and brother Holly were born there. They then moved to Seattle where Sam attended the Seattle Pacific School, now Seattle Pacific University. Finally, sometime in the early 1900s they headed up to Alaska, stopping off at Skagway for a time, finally making their way to the Old Iliamna Village in 1903 where Baard settled with his wife and sons. They are listed on the Old Iliamna Village 1910 census, Sam is 21 and Holly is 15. They lived across the river from the village. Baard was in the freighting business. Sam and Holly married half-sisters, Sophie and Lagaria. Sam and Sophie were the first to settle over in Pedro Bay. Sam was the Commissioner of the Iliamna Lake Area. He also ran a store there in Pedro Bay. It was a focal point in the area. His children have said that there were many people coming and going. They also fostered many children because so many were orphaned by illness and accidents. See Appendix No. 5 for more on their wives and children.

17. The Old Iliamna Village School opened in 1908 and closed in 1932. It ran for 24 years.

18. Anna's parents were literate. At least her Dad, William Rickteroff was. He also spoke three languages; English, Russian, and Dena'ina. So it is interesting that Walter says his Mom couldn't read and spoke only Dena'ina. One wonders if this was by choice. Valun, Anna's youngest sister, mentions in *Our Stories Our Lives* that her Dad would speak in Russian to his sister, Daria. Valun says they didn't pay attention and didn't try to learn that language (Russian).

19. Buck Delkettie mentions the gardens in his *Anchorage Daily News* 1/25/2004 interview. He said while they spent their summers in the fish camp at the mouth of the Iliamna River, they had to go back up to the village several times to weed and water the gardens. He said he disliked this chore.

20. See Appendix No. 5 on Michael C. Rickteroff.

21. David Victoroff is the son of Michael C Rickteroff and his wife Katherine Simeon. When Michael C died, Katherine married Mike Jensen. David said when they lived with Mike Jensen it wasn't very good. They always seemed to live in a very small place with too many people. He never had a bed but would sleep curled up behind the stove to stay warm. His Mom died, when he was 6 or 7. He then went to live with his Grandpa Nikita Simeon. His grandpa died in a house fire shortly after. David then had to go and live with his Aunt Hilda who was married to a Chester Burke. They lived in Goose Bay. Chester was a trapper. His Aunt Hilda got sick with TB. Chester took her to a sanatorium in Palmer where she died in childbirth. Chester was left with two daughters, Katherine and Francis, and David. He put the two daughters into an orphanage in Valdez. He put David into a boarding school in Eklutna. It was here that David's name was misspelled. Apparently Chester couldn't say his r's and so David's name came out as Victoroff instead of Rickteroff. David wasn't aware of this for a long time. He was sent from Eklutna to Seward, then to Mt. Edgecumbe where he completed high school. The two girls married military men and David lost track of them.

22. See Note No. 14 under section *Walter, On His Own* and Appendix No. 4 for more on Charlie Jensen and son, Mike Jensen.

23. Elizabeth (born 1912) does show up on the 1930 Iliamna Lake Census as wife of Mike Jensen, age 18. They have two children listed, Freda – age 2 and Carl –age 1. This would mean she was married to Mike by 1928 or so. Both her parents are listed as Kenai, meaning they were both Dena'ina. According to oral history she was a ward of Cusma Rikterov and his wife, Mariia. See Appendix No. 2 for more on Cusma (Kos'ma) and his second wife Mariia Malaku b. 1872, a Dena'ina of the Old Iliamna Village. She married him September 16, 1890, died April 19, 1909 in childbirth. She had 7 children, most died very young, the others are not mentioned or don't show up with Cusma in the 1910 census so it may be assumed they either died or were adopted. Only one ward is listed, a Petr Biou, b. ca. 1884 or 1901.

    The problem with Elizabeth being a ward of Cusma and Mariia is that Mariia is already dead before Elizabeth is even born, since Mariia died in 1909 and Elizabeth is born in 1912. Cusma did remarry in 1910 to a Dariia (b.1889) but Elizabeth does not show up on the census with them. One possibility could be that she was older than 18 in 1930. (This from oral history, Ardnt's notes and Census records)

24. On Mike Jensen's Boat getting destroyed: Rose Hedlund remembers that winter of 1941 as being very mild and the lake didn't freeze that winter. She said it was the year they built the FAA in Iliamna and when Mike's boat got wrecked by the sudden East windstorm. From interview with Rose Hedlund, 12/7/03.

25. Walter told this story with a funny grin on his face. An Alusha Kolyaha shows up on the 1920 census. Birthyear of 1878. He is listed as a widow at age 42 with a daughter named Sofia Kolyaha. Sofia Kolyaha shows up on the Old Iliamna Village school attendance records from 1912 to 1923. Not sure the connection between Alusha and Alex Kolyaha (b. 1859) who was Nick Kolyaha's (b. July 1890) father.

26. Russell Merrill (1894-1929) an Alaskan aviation pioneer was the first pilot into many rural locations, including Old Iliamna Village. Merrill Airport (est. 1930) was named after him as was Merrill Pass. This is the Pass where his plane disappeared in 1929.

27. Ignatia Delkettie (b. September 1903) shows up in the 1910 census under the household of an Evon Delkettie (b. 1859). Mother listed as Maria (b. July 1873). Her place of birth and that of her parents is just listed as Alaska. Interesting note on the listing; there are two other children listed, but Ignatia's father is listed as from Kustatan while the father of the other two children is listed as from Iliamna (Old Iliamna Village). Ignatia is also listed on the school attendance lists from 1909 to 1923. He married Annie Balluta of Nondalton and moved there.

28. On the church building: According to *Through Orthodox Eyes* the Alaska Russian Church Archives record (ARCA) states this about the church in the Old Iliamna Village: "In Iliamna, an inland Dena'ina village rarely visited by missionaries, the first prayer house consecrated after St. Nicholas was built in 1877 by Savva Riktorov, and six years later was rebuilt anew by residents themselves, who maintained the building and in 1907 renovated it" (page 40). You can compare this picture with that of the picture of the church in Hannah Breece's book on page 117 before the church was moved.

Walter, On His Own

1. Note on comment by Walter's Mom, "there were a lot of white men in the Old Iliamna Village." The 1910 & 1920 census supports this statement. Of the 91 people listed in the 1910 census, 25 are from outside of Alaska, many from Norway and Denmark. Of the 75 enrolled in the 1920 census, 22 are from someplace other than Alaska. Hannah Breece who was there from 1909 –1911 stated in her memoir, "the village consisted of about 150 souls, including four Danes,

one German, one Swede, one Frenchman and four American men." Her nearest neighbor was an "aged Danish recluse" that she never got to know because he stayed to himself.

2. I have been unable to find any other information on Alfred Johnson, Walter's Dad. He lived a solitary life on Branch River. Apparently he fell through the ice one winter in 1948/49.

3. On Buck (Drafim) Delkettie: Buck lived with Walter there at Lonesome Bay until he turned 18, then he spent the winter with Holly and Lagaria Foss in Pedro Bay. Holly Foss was Buck's biological Dad. Buck was called into the army that same year, and spent the next four years in the army. He then worked at the Jonesville coal mine near Sutton for a while, spent the winter with Nels Hedlund in Dillingham, who he had met while in the army, and fished with him that summer. The next summer he fished with Hugh Millet and married Hugh's daughter, Jessie in 1947. From then on he and Jessie lived in Anchorage. He made his living as a plumber. (This information from an article appearing in *Anchorage Daily News* January 25, 2004.)

4. Frank Rickteroff (1922-1960) was the son of Evon Rickteroff (1892-1951) and a Stepanita of Nondalton. He was the brother of Lolla who married Walter's brother Nicolai and Lillian who married an Ed Kahn then George Lapp. Frank married Phina Carlsen. He drowned by falling off Holly and Lagaria Foss's dock in Pedro Bay.

5. Mary Balluta was the granddaughter of Marpha Rikhterov (b. January 30, 1894), Marpha was the daughter of Evfimii Rikterov. See Appendix No. 2. Marfa Rikhterov married Nicolai Grigor'ev Nicolai on February 28, 1916 and had a daughter Marfa and a son, Gory Nicolai. Marfa must have died by 1920 as Nicolai Grigor'ev is listed in the 1920 Census as a widow. Gory Nicolai was Virginia Jensen's second husband. Marfa Nicolai, Mary's Mom married Mike Balluta who

died from T.B. before Mary was born. Mary says she was born in Eagle Bay. Marfa then married a Steve Hobson and had Luther Hobson, Mary's half-brother. Her mom died when she was about 2 years old. Mary was then raised by Agafia or Mrs. Singka, her great grandmother in Pedro Bay. Her brother Luther was raised by his Dad's relatives in Nondalton.

6. Mary told me a great story about her Great Grandma Agafia. Apparently Agafia was from a Dena'ina Village near Lime Village, possibly Stony River or one of the Mulchatna Villages. Agafia's family often went down to the Bristol Bay coast to try to get seafood in the spring when there was so little to eat in the interior. While her family was there on this one trip, influenza was going on and all of her family died, leaving Agafia alone. Effim (Epheme) Rickteroff happened to be traveling down that way. He found her and took her home to Old Iliamna Village with him. Agafia was still too young to marry so Effim had his aunt, Daria Rickteroff take care of her. Daria taught her how to sew and cook. Then when she was 16 she and Effim married. (From interview with Mary Jensen.)

She is listed in the confessionals as Agafiia Byktaiutna, a Kenaika born 1874, married September 16, 1890 at age 16. She and Effim had six children – four lived to adulthood: Ioann (Evon)-b. June 15, 1892, Marfa – b. January 30, 1894 and married Nikolai Grigor'ev (3rd wife) at age 20, Stephen – b. August 1899, Varvara (Vera) – born January 3, 1907. (This information is from Katherine Ardnt's notes.)

Hannah Breece describes Agafia as: "a handsome, intelligent woman". Hannah had a squirrel skin robe made for her by Agafia. *A Schoolteacher in Old Alaska: The Story of Hannah Breece* by Jane Jacobs, pages 95 and 113. There is also a photo of Effim and Agafia in this book.

7. World War II was between 1939 and 1945. The Japanese bombed Pearl Harbor December 7, 1941. They invaded the Aleutian Islands of Attu and Kiska, on June 3, 1942.

8. Dolly Foss and George G. Jacko lived in Lonesome Bay for part of 1949-50. Then Benny Foss and Agnes Jacko also lived there for a winter, after they were married. Dolly said Pedro Bay did not have any houses for them. Nicolai Jensen's house in Lonesome Bay was still okay to live in.

9. The US Bureau of Fisheries put out a Dolly Varden tail bounty between 1921 and 1940. It was thought that the Dolly Varden, an arctic char fish was the cause of the diminished salmon runs. After a time it was realized that most of the tails that came in were from either trout or salmon. The program was finally shut down.

10. Hans Seversen (1870-1939) shows up in the 1910 census of Old Iliamna Village. He is shown as single, b. December 1869 in Dakota (1930 census says Minnesota), with parents both born in Norway. No occupation listed. He shows up again in the 1930 Iliamna Lake Census with a wife Madrona from Nondalton and children listed as: George-age 17, Mary-age 15, Edward-age 12, Annie-age 10, Alexandria-age 9, Martin-age 4, Walter-age 1. The children also show up on the Old Iliamna Village School attendance records in 1927, 1928, and 1930. His wife is also listed as Yenlu Nudlash Brooks from Nondalton in *Through Orthodox Eyes*. Branson provides much more information on Hans and his wife Yenlu in *Seversen's Roadhouse: Crossroads of Bristol Bay, Alaska*.

11. Evon Rickteroff (b. 15 June 1892 – d. spring of 1951) was the son of Epheme (Efim)(1859-1911?) and Agafia Rickteroff. (See Appendix 2 on Efim.)

    Evon had a son, Manuel with Annie Delkettie (1911-). She was the daughter of Garrella and Mariia Rickteroff (1889-1930s?) Delkettie. Mariia was Walter's aunt, his Mom, Anna's younger sister. See Appendix 3 for more on Mariia.

    Evon had a daughter, Lolla with another woman. No one remembers who this was. Lolla married Nicolai Jensen and died of TB a couple years later.

Evon then married a Stepanita of Nondalton. They had Lillian, Frank, and Evon. Lillian married Ed Kahn and had two children; Irene and William. After Ed died she married George Lapp. Frank married Phina Carlson, daughter of Fedosia Carlson. No information on Evon, the youngest son.

Evon left Old Iliamna Village and built a house in Pedro Bay on the shore close to where Pauline Roehl's house is located. That was where he died.

12. On *bivak*: This word is apparently of Russian origin. I got the spelling from Jim Kari's *Dena'ina Topical Dictionary*, page 292.

13. See Appendix No. 4.

14. On Charlie Jensen: Carl (Charlie) Jensen born in Copenhagen, Denmark on June 1879 arrived in the US in 1900. Story is that he left home at the age of 7 as a cabin boy. He shows up on the 1910 Iliamna Census at age 31 married to Anna with two sons listed, Michael-age 4 and George-age 1. George must have died as there is no further mention of him. He left Annie and moved down to live on the Kvichak above Levelock. Alma Jacko said that her Dad wanted her to go and live in his house when he realized that he needed to leave because of his health. She didn't want to so he burned his house down before leaving the country. It was thought that he died at the Pioneers home in Sitka. I did check the records and found two Carl Jensens listed. One, Carl E. with a birth date as 09/01/1881 and death as 08/27/1952 at the age of 71 entered the home in 1908. The second, Carl F. with birth date as 01/18/1873 and death as 06/06/1964 at the age of 91 entered the home in 1903. I don't think either of these guys were Charlie Jensen as he didn't leave Levelock until sometime in the 1930s. Walter remembers that he and his brothers would stop to visit Charlie when they were on their way to Bristol Bay. Walter was 14 when he started going to Bristol Bay. He remembers Charlie as being a very old man and that he didn't even commercial fish anymore by that time. Charlie was actually only 57 then but he may have been frail due to ill health.

15. See Appendix No. 2 for more on Epheme (Efim), also Endnotes No. 5 & 6 for more on Marfa and Agafia.

16. Victor was sent to Naknek for a while, perhaps because that is where his mother, Virginia was. He was brought back to Pedro Bay and lived for a time with Gus and Mary, finally ending up with Gillie and Alma.

17. According to *Seversen's Roadhouse: Crossroads Of Bristol Bay, Alaska* the Seversens either lived in Nondalton or Iliamna. In this book Bailey makes the statement that Hans Seversen's kids never went to school. However, Walter remembers that they did live for a time at the Old Iliamna village. The kids also show up on the school attendance records of the Old Iliamna Village School. Year 1927 : George-age 16 and Mary-age 14. 1928: George, Mary, & Edward-age 12. Year 1932: George-age 20, Mary-age 17, Edward-age14, Annie-age 12, Alexandria-age 8.

18. Effim Karshekoff was the son of Martha Kovoliak and a Karshekoff of Eagle Bay. Karshekoff was Donkoo's son that Walter spoke of earlier.

19. Alexander Flymn was a Norwegian born October 1878 in Norway. He appears on the 1910 Old Iliamna Village Census at the age of 32. He is said to have helped build the school in the village, which must have been 1906 or 1907. He married Anna, the ward of Aleksei and Wasalisa Rickterov in 1904 but Anna is not listed with him in the 1910 census. Also see Appendix No. 4. Alex Flymn, Jr is his son. Alex Flymn, Jr. lived in Pile Bay for a short time then they moved to Homer where he ran a barge service between Homer and Iliamna Bay.

Left Lonesome Bay

1. Note: Nick Kolyaha refers to a location in Iliamna Bay, 'Qanlcha Nut'. "When they used to hunt sea otter, that's where the women used to stay."

   From an interview by Jim Kari (4-2-81), translated by Andrew Balluta.

2. Annie's first husband, Trygve Olsen, realized he was getting sick. Apparently, he spoke of this to Sam Foss, Annie's brother-in-law. He was concerned about being a burden. So he decided it was best if he left and went someplace that he could be cared for. (From interview with Dolly Foss Jacko)

3. Dick Mysee (b. January 1889) shows up on the 1910 and 1920 Old Iliamna Village census. His mother is listed as Faramia Mysee, she was born March of 1850 in Mulchatna. Dick's father's birthplace is listed as Lake Clark.

4. Sophus Hendrickson shows up on the 1910 Old Iliamna Village census. He was born in Norway in October 1889, and was a cousin of Baard Foss. Hollie Foss mentions him several times in his diary entries of 1921.

5. "Aleut" is a term used to designate either the Yupik or Alutiq people. It is of Russian origin. Today the term more accurately designates the people of the Aleutian Islands.

6. "Dagos" This was a term used for those fishermen that came from the Lower '48 and were of Italian blood. According to the Wikipedia: *"Dago is a US ethnic slur for Italians and a UK ethnic slur for Italians, Spanish/Hispanics or Latin Americans."* According to Webster: *"Dago comes from 'Diego' a common Spanish name, and is usually used disparagingly towards a person of Italian or Spanish descent."* Walter uses it to designate a certain group of people, much like he uses the term 'Aleut' not meaning it to be derogatory. It was a common usage.

7. Donald Stump and his wife Lorene were missionaries in Pile Bay from 1945 to 1957. They spent several years in Iliamna where he started the summer camp program and spring conference. Both events were moved to Tanalian (Port Alsworth). The Stumps moved to Anchorage where he started the program called Native New Life. This was an outreach to all the village people that came to Anchorage. They met every Monday night. There is a book *Alaska ….New Life for an Ancient People* by Lloyd Mattson that tells his rather incredible story. When Walter speaks of Don, it is with great fondness.

8. Walter was very skilled with the guitar. He and Annie often sang duets at services, either in church, Native New Life Meetings, or at the Spring Conferences held in Port Alsworth. He was generally the lead guitarist at these gatherings. He often got together with other musicians.

9. Bill Duray (1860-1949/50) is listed as William E. Duryea born in New York on the 1920 census. An Elbert Duryea (1850-?) is listed with him. William shows up again on the 1930 census. He had a place in Cottonwood Bay, which is one bay over from Iliamna Bay to the west. When he first came into the country he worked with Ed McKinnet with his freighting business. Apparently he would walk all the way from Cottonwood Bay to meet the boats that came into Iliamna Bay, about 7 miles at low tide. He then joined a Dutton and worked a silver/copper mine up by Moose Lake above Cottonwood Bay. Duray married but his wife moved back to New York and Duray would go and visit her but for the most part stayed in Cottonwood Bay so he could work the mine. He was known as "Uncle Bill" to Carl William and his children. It seems he was not their actual "uncle" but a distant relative. (Information from 1920 Census, telephone conversation with Linda Williams)

10. Evon Kovoliac shows up on the 1930 Iliamna Lake Census. He is listed as an Aleut living in Newhalen with his wife and three children. His age is 35.

11. Dick Mishakoff (b. March 4, 1894 – d. December 1964) was a lay reader for the Russian Orthodox Church. He was originally from Kenai but had moved to Tyonek. His brother Nick (Nikita) (b. April 30, 1905) lived in Kenai. According to church records Nick died on November 11, 1969 and was buried in Kenai. There was no record of Dick's death so it may be assumed he died and was buried there at Tyonek. According to the Kenai Russian Orthodox records Dick was a lay reader not a priest of the church.

12. Emma Roehl (b. 1920) was the daughter of Frederick J. Roehl, Sr. (b. 1860 d. 1924) and his wife Mary (b. 1912) of Koggiung. They lived in the Old Iliamna Village.

13. Ole Wasenkari (March 4, 1899 – June 1, 1984) shows up on the 1930 Iliamna Census with his older brother, Walter. Shows both were born in Washington State. Their parents were both from Finland. Walter was 34, and Ole was 30. They list themselves as trappers. Ole's last known residence was King Salmon, AK.

14. Mary Seversen was the daughter of Hans Seversen and Yenlu of Roadhouse or what is now called Iliamna. See note No. 4 in *Walter, On His Own*.

15. Nels Hedlund was from Bethel. He married Rose Kinney and settled in Chekok, the homestead she inherited from her Dad, Jack Kinney.

16. Note on "Living On the Kvichak". Early that fall Jack Vantrease came by on his way from Bristol Bay to Pile Bay on Iliamna Lake. He suggested to Walter and Annie that Trygve and Ethel go to Pile Bay with him so that they could attend the school there. Ethel said she remembered being very excited as she always wanted to go to school. So they went with the Vantreases to Pile Bay. Ethel stayed with the Vantrease family while Tryve stayed with the teacher.

17. For more on Ignasia Delkettie see note No. 28 on *Walter's Early Life*.

18. Victory Bible High School was located on Mile 95 of the Palmer Highway. It was a boarding high school for rural high school students. It has closed.

19. Barney Furman was a missionary with Arctic Missions/Interact Missions. He spent several years in the late 60s with his wife Ruth and three children in Pedro Bay.

20. Note on Ernie Zink: Born 2-3-1894. Died 7-1-70. Ernie lived in E-Z Bay on the west side of Pedro Bay. He got sick in the 60s with cancer and went back to California for treatment. When he realized he wasn't going to get better he sold his place in Pedro Bay and returned to California where he died.

21. Carl Williams operated the freight service at Iliamna Bay and maintained the road between Iliamna Bay and Pile Bay. His son Raymond Williams continues this business. They also haul fishing boats over the road. This is a shortcut between Cook Inlet and Bristol Bay.

22. Note on 'bones'. This is a term used to refer to the spine of the salmon. The salmon was gutted, and filleted off the spine. This part, the spine, generally still had a lot of flesh on it. Two of these were then tied together and hung to air dry on an outside rack – some people smoked them. But this was a main food supply for the dogs. When Walter says 100 'bones' he probably means 200, because they are two tied together creating one unit.

23. Walter's youngest daughter, Ruthie married Lanny Andree of Dillingham. They lived several years there at Tommy Pt. after Walter and Annie moved to Homer.

Camping, Trapping, Hunting

1. See Note from *Left Alone*, No. 9 on Fedosia.

2. See Appendix No. 5 on Wassalissa (Vasilissa).

3. On long distance running: Gillie Jacko once told me about how as a young man he was required to run long distances on little or nothing to eat. He said he was trained to do that. There is an interesting reference to this by Alfred B. Schanz. He and his party while on an exploration trip in 1891 traveling from the Nushagak toward Lake Clark ran into this young man, described as such. "a handsome, well-built, athletic-looking young fellow, with fine, velvety black eyes and a laughing, rosy-cheeked, reddish-brown complexion. . . after he found that we could not understand him, started off on a graceful run ahead of our dogs evidently to show us the way to his village." This young man eventually led the Schanz party to his village while running ahead of them. (*Lake Clark, Lake Iliamna Country* Alaska Geographic Quarterly, Vol. 13, No. 4. 1986.)

4. Steven Sours (Sava) was a Dena'ina man that lived in Eagle Bay. He had a trapping cabin there at Talarik Creek. There were several Sours living at Eagle Bay. Walter didn't know if they were related to his brother Grasim Sours. There were also some Sours that show up on the school attendance records of the Old Iliamna Village School. They are often referred to as Sava instead of Sours.

5. Effim Karshekoff was the son of Donkoo Karshekoff of Eagle Bay. His mom was Martha, the daughter of Joluk Zacarooska and his wife Nastashia of Old Iliamna Village. Annie Kay Karshekoff was his sister, she was the third wife of Mike Jensen.

6. Note on Sam Murray: (1895? -1940?). Born in New York State. A Bristol Bay fisherman, trapper and miner. Married Annie Olsen of South Naknek. From *Seversen's Roadhouse: Crossroads of Bristol Bay, Alaska*. Edited by John Branson.

7. A Wien Air Alaska airplane Fairchild F-27B crashed at Pedro Bay into Foxie's Lake. All 39 on board died. Cause is said to be structural failure due to stress fractures and severe turbulence. The plane was on its way from Anchorage to Dillingham.

8. Arthur and Willis were the sons of Fred and Vera Roehl. Fred was the son of Frederick Roehl. See note from section II, number 6 on Frederick J Roehl, Sr. Vera (b. January 3, 1907) was the daughter of Efim and Agafia Rickterov.

   Arthur was adopted and raised by his aunt Sophie (b. 1906), who was married to Walter's oldest brother Grasim. After Grasim died she married Hans Seversen, of Iliamna Roadhouse. Hans died in 1939. She then moved to Dillingham where she met and married Penman and they moved to Homer. This is where Arthur grew up.

Commercial Fishing In Bristol Bay

1. There always seemed to have been some type of store in Old Iliamna Village. This would make sense if Savva Rickterov did 'start' the village for a Russian fur company. It is also noted in the historical section of *Lake Clark, Lake Iliamna Country* that "The Foss family opened a store in 1903, Peter Anderson established one in 1904, and Fred J. Roehl, Sr, had a store and was the postmaster in Old Iliamna by 1913."

2. On Paul Cusma of Nondalton. He was the son of Maxim Cusma and Yevenia Sava. Yevenia was the daughter of Pete Sava and Dolly Micey. (Nondalton Genealogy 1985 Draft)

3. Simmie Zachar was the son of Homoshka Zachar. Simmie shows up on the Old Iliamna Village school enrollment of 1932 listed as age 15, so his birthyear would have been 1917, five years older than Walter. He married a lady from Kokhanok and settled there.

4. Frank DeSilva was married to Nora Flymn (b. 12/24/1923). She was the daughter of Alec and Annie Flymn. Frank and Nora lived for a while at her folks old place there in Kokhanok Bay then moved to Homer.

5. See note on 'Dagos'. *Left Lonesome Bay*, No. 6.

6. James Rickteroff was the son of William Mike Rickterof (see Appendix No. 3) and Annie John (see Note 2, under *Left Alone*).

7. Benny Foss was the son of Sam and Sophie (Rickterof) Foss. (See Appendix No. 5) He married Agnes Jacko, daughter of Gillie and Alma Jacko. Ben and Agnes had 5 children: Ben Jr., Laverne, Leonard, Glen, Ronnie, and Connie. They moved to Oregon and raised their family there.

8. This information is out of sync with what Walter recalls later of the change over from sailboats to powerboats and selling his converted boat. However, Trygve's age is right because he was 12 in 1949. So it may be two separate events he is remembering here.

9. Rose Hedlund was the daughter of Jack Kinney and Eleana Balluta. Rose married Nels Hedlund of Bethel, AK. He is the uncle of Ron and Norman Aaberg of Pedro Bay.

10. Johnny Kankaton is from Nondalton.

11. pewed: This word can be found in the *Dictionary of Newfoundland English*.

    It is of French origin – pieu. A pew is "a long stick with a sharp prong or tine affixed to the end, used in moving fish from boat to fishing-stage."

12. Josh Earl Jacko is the son of Norman M. Jacko, who is the son of George and Dolly (Foss) Jacko. George is the son of Gillie and Alma (Jensen) Jacko-see Appendix No. 4.) Dolly Foss Jacko is the daughter of Sam and Sophie (Rickterov) Foss. See Appendix No. 5.

13. Fred Roehl is the son of Arthur Roehl and Pauline Kolyaha. Arthur was the son of Fred and his first wife Vera. Pauline was the daughter of Alec and Zenia (Zachar) Kolyaha.

Final Years In Homer

1. I went online and searched the internet for this term but could find nothing. When I mentioned the term to my husband he knew what it was. I may not be spelling it correctly – did try several other spellings but no results.

2. Babe and Mary Alsworth are from Port Alsworth. Babe was a legendary pilot of the Iliamna Lake Area. Mary ran the post office and weather station there at Port Alsworth. He and Mary retired and moved over to Hawaii.

3. This is the "The Friendship Center." They took Annie four times a week for four hours each time.

4. The ladies that came in were hired from the Homer Health Center. The Alzheimer's Association out of Anchorage also provided some help for Annie.